ONE S___ _____

ONE STEP AHEAD

David J. Azrieli (Azrylewicz), Memoirs: 1939–1950

Written by

DANNA J. AZRIELI

Yad Vashem • Jerusalem • 2001

Editor: Leah Aharonov

ISBN — 965–308–125–X
© Yad Vashem, 2001
First published as *Tza'ad Ehad Lefanim*, 1999
Printed by Daf Noy, Jerusalem

This book is dedicated to the memory of my parents,
Raphael-Hirsch
and
Sara-Chaya,
to
my brother Pinchas
and my sister Tzireleh

who perished in the Holocaust

Table of Contents

Preface

Everyone who survived the war has a story to tell but throughout my childhood, the story of my father's escape from Nazi-occupied Poland in 1939 was shrouded in mystery. In fact, he rarely spoke of his life as a child or of how he survived the war and arrived in Palestine in 1942.

Occasionally, he would tell a small part of his story... like the time he had to run across the top of a moving train to save his life, or the time he embarked upon his first capitalist venture by selling butter in Siberia. Each story he told, however, seemed to stand alone. I could never figure out what had happened first, or how one event was related to another. Often, just when I thought I had the whole sequence of events figured out, my father would tell a *new story*.

When he would begin to speak, all movement around the dinner table stopped. He told us about the Uzbeki couple who helped find him a job, or the time he worked in a flour mill in a small village located in the former Soviet Union. I would hang on to every word, consciously suspending my need to piece the events together in order to understand the overall story. I was simply grateful that he was in the mood to talk and I knew that any distraction might make him stop.

Sometimes when my siblings and I would press for more details, my father would disclose selected bits of information that only served to make us more curious. He would remember that his mother, Sarah, was a brave woman who believed in forming a Jewish state. He also often mentioned her delicious homemade raspberry jams and liqueur. Or he would refer to his father, Raphael, a busy, successful businessman who always provided well for his family. While these descriptions of his parents — my grandparents — were always vague and never enough to satisfy our intense curiosity, we dared not ask for any more details for fear of upsetting him or reminding him of his loss.

Finally, in 1990, my father decided to return to Poland and tell the stories of his past. My sister, Naomi, was living in Europe at the time, and I had just finished college, so the two of us were free to accompany him on this journey. My mother, Stephanie, my sister Sharon, and my brother Rafi were unable to join us, but we promised to videotape everything and to return with many details and stories.

During this journey to Poland and Russia, I was overwhelmed by my need to hear all the details of my father's escape in a way that made sense — from beginning to end. I felt as though this "untold story" was the missing link that would finally explain my family. Throughout the trip, Naomi and I asked for specific facts of every event and, to my surprise, my father was willing to tell us more than ever before. We taped conversations while poring over maps, driving in the car, riding trains, and eating dinner. Finally, the story of what had happened from when he first left Poland in September 1939, to his arrival in Palestine in September 1942 started taking the shape of this memoir.

Seven years after I started this project, my father asked me to extend the story to include his arrival in Palestine and the years leading up to the War of Independence. After hours and hours of more interviews, the story of his life during the years he spent working, studying, and participating in the fight for a Jewish homeland began to unfold. The themes that reveal themselves throughout the story indicate that there is much more to David J. Azrieli than is obvious in the presentation of his public self. In the business world, he is known for his toughness and acumen, so it might be a surprise to learn of his boyhood idealism and concern for social justice. It is slightly less surprising, however, when viewed in the context of his commitment to Jewish philanthropic organizations and his mother's commitment to Zionism.

My father's youthful excitement over the ideals that formed the basis for socialist governments is entirely consistent with his curious nature and constant willingness to explore new ideas. It is also consistent with his determination to survive. He was drawn to the Soviet Union at a time when the political climate in Russian-occupied Poland still permitted him to maintain his liberty — and when his youthful quest for social justice coincided with his pursuit for self-preservation.

I would be remiss if I did not also acknowledge that in

every survival story there is also a component of luck... but often, moments of luck are also coupled with intuition. No one will ever know if it was luck or insight when he made the decision to leave a town before the Nazis descended upon it. Also, throughout the story, my father recalls many Jewish and non-Jewish people who were particularly kind to him. Often, a stranger's willingness to help him catch a ride on a wagon or disguise him as an Arab peasant made the difference between his life and death. This ability to make friends and rely upon them in a time of crisis...was it pure luck, or was there also an element of foresight?

Finally, I find my father's continual appreciation of nature, music, and architecture — even while running for his life — to be a particularly unique element in this story. He is constantly noting the variety of architectural styles and remarking on the soothing and inspiring effects of a beautiful piece of music or a live symphony orchestra. This ability to see and appreciate the beauty around him is in noticeable contrast to the lack of detail he has offered about the emotional connections he must have felt with his siblings, parents, or with people he encountered along his way.

Over the years, I have asked for more of these kinds of emotional descriptions and information, but what my father has not conveyed to me, I cannot convey to you. I am simply "the keeper" of this tale. My father is the teller. My goal in writing it all down, for him, is to make sure that the first part of the story of his life is preserved for anyone who wants to hear it. To do this effectively, I have made the decision to write in my father's voice. After attempting many other techniques, I realized that writing in the first person was the most appropriate method of conveying this story, since this is how I have heard it over the years. Finally, the time has come to tell this amazing tale of perseverance. I offer this book as a gift to my father in return for his many lessons in survival and determination — and for his absolute and unconditional love.

I would like to express my sincere appreciation to my cousin, Helen Pianka Binik, for her invaluable editorial and substantive comments, her time, effort and patience in reading the many drafts that this memoir has seen over the years. I would also like to thank my sister, Naomi, for her emotional support, and for her historical and editorial comments, without which this project may never have been completed. I would also like to thank my mother, Stephanie Azrieli, my sister Sharon Azrieli, Myer Bick, Gil Troy, Linda Adams, Menachem Einan, Ada and Michael Shusheim, Nancy Rosenzweig, and Adam and Isabella Gillon for taking the time to read this memoir and help see this process to its final and successful completion. Finally, I would like to thank Avner Shalev, Bella Gutterman, and all the other people at Yad Vashem who made this project possible. Thank you, thank you, thank you.

Danna J. Azrieli

Prologue

The first time I returned to Poland after the war was in 1980. Forty-one years earlier, in 1939, I had left the safety of my childhood home to live as a refugee and, for all of those years, I had no desire to return to the country of my youth. Poland was part of my past, and I saw no reason to revisit it. I also make no apologies for the anger I feel toward the Polish people who participated in destroying millions of Jewish lives. Hitler's extermination camps could not have existed on Polish soil without a population willing to live next door, and so, over the years, I have successfully disassociated myself from any connection I have to the country, its language, or its culture.

When I did return to Poland in 1980, I was focused on how pleased I was because of how far I had come over the years. Since the war, I have attained economic and social success, I have made significant contributions to the Canadian and Israeli economies, and I have a beautiful family. There could be no claim of a Nazi or Polish victory over me.

Ten years after my first return visit, in 1990, I decided to go back again. This time I traveled with my two youngest daughters, Naomi and Danna, and my goal was to tell the stories of my childhood and how I survived as a refugee during World War II. On this trip I wanted not only to emphasize the horrors of the war, but also to remember the joys of my youth, my family, and the events that transpired after my parents sent my brothers and me away to escape the Nazis half a century ago.

Upon arriving in Warsaw, my children and I went directly to the Hotel Victoria, where I had arranged to meet a driver for our travels around the Polish countryside. My plan was to visit my hometown, Makow Mazowiecki (Makow), and roughly follow the same route I had taken as a seventeen-year-old boy upon the outbreak of the war.

Within an hour of our arrival, our driver came to meet us at the hotel. He greeted me in Polish and, for the first time in fifty years, I decided to respond in kind. Ever since the war, I have associated the Polish language with sheer hatred and destruction. In fact, it had been so long since I had uttered a Polish syllable that I was surprised to see how easily the words came out of my mouth. In semi-fluent Polish I arranged to meet the driver for an early morning departure to Makow. I wanted to spend our first day following the eastern route I had outlined on our map in blue, while stopping in every small town I had passed in September 1939. I also planned digressions from this route in order to visit the concentration camps Treblinka, Auschwitz, and Birkenau.

The next morning, we drove along the familiar road from Warsaw to Makow. The road has been modernized and is now a two-lane highway, occasionally blocked by a slow-moving tractor or wagon. In 1937, I attended school in Warsaw and was driven on this road many times. From the car window I could still smell the white pine trees, which reminded me of the terrible homesickness I had felt during that year in school. Then, as now, the road was framed by trees so dense on top that barely any sun reaches the ground below. As I looked up at the tall white pines, I remembered that the earth beneath them was mossy and dry. Delicious edible mushrooms grow in this moss and, every summer, when my family used to travel a few kilometers away from Makow and vacation in an old farmer's cottage at the edge of the forest, my mother would go outside after the rain and pick these mushrooms for supper.

From the early Middle Ages, the town of Makow flourished as a thriving business city with an active commercial market located in the central square. Every Tuesday and Friday, farmers and artisans from the surrounding areas would bring their goods for trade. The success of the market was also due, in part, to the town's proximity to the Orzyc River, which provided easy access to Warsaw. The total population of Makow was approximately 12,000, of which about 6,500 were Jewish and the remainder Catholic. Geographically, the town was divided between the Jewish and Catholic communities. The Jewish section was dominated by a large synagogue, and the Polish section by a grand Gothic cathedral. The communities lived in relative harmony with each other despite the obvious separation. Jewish and Polish children attended separate schools, and adults rarely met, except for trading and other official business.

When we arrived in Makow, the driver parked in the center of town in front of the market square. My family had lived on the second floor of a house on the corner of this square. The original, three-story building was made of stone and was finished with colored stucco and it had a backyard where we used to park a horse and buggy. The building standing on the corner today is not the one I lived in. It must have been demolished during the war. When I was a boy, there was a pump in the middle of the square that provided water to the town's residents. Every day — sometimes twice a day — the water carrier would deliver water for cooking, drinking, and washing. Today, a decorative fountain stands in its place, and the square has been converted into a park.

My daughters and I walked around the main streets while I looked for the landmarks of my youth. We saw the cinema where I used to sneak inside and watch Shirley Temple movies, the candy store where I bought chocolate, and the houses where my relatives used to live. Everything seemed smaller and closer together than I remembered. When I was a boy, the walk to synagogue used to feel painfully long, but now I could look down the street where the synagogue used to be and I realized that it was only a few blocks from the center of town. In fact, although there was no trace of the building, the street name had not changed: Bozniczna, "Synagogue Street."

The synagogue was an exquisite building built of brick and mortar. The entrance was a magnificent hall lined with stained-glass windows with a staircase on either side of the door. Both sides of the stairs were decorated with musical instruments made from chiseled wood and painted in gold and white so they looked like shiny metal. At the top of the staircases, there was a series of separate prayer rooms called *shteeblach*, where different groups and professional guilds would pray. At the end of the hall was a gallery for women, who sat separately from men during services.

The main sanctuary was enormous, with a ceiling almost forty feet high and a magnificent chandelier hanging in the middle. The ceiling was painted the color of the sky, with clouds and a glowing sun that seemed to give light by day and night. There were also stars and flying angels painted in blue, green, purple, and gold. Candelabras hung between the *bima* (altar) and the *Aron ha-Kodesh* (Holy Ark) and, on either side of the Holy Ark, there were sculptures of two lions holding tablets engraved with the Ten Commandments. The Torah Scrolls (the books of the Old Testament) inside the Holy Ark were wrapped in mantles made of velvet and silk. These mantles had beautiful designs of holiday scenes embroidered in silver and gold by women from the community. As a child, I spent many hours daydreaming in the midst of this beauty.

Today, all of it is gone.

What stunned me most was the new soccer field in what used to be the Jewish cemetery. A stone path led to the field but, if you looked closely, you saw they were not ordinary cobblestones but Jewish tombstones. I could see Hebrew letters and the occasional Star of David facing upward. Once again, I was overwhelmed with anger. My father's family had lived in Makow for hundreds of years. My great-great-grandparents had been buried in this cemetery and I had hoped to find a gravestone with a familiar name. Every trace of the Jewish community I had known had been destroyed by the Nazis.

We walked around the streets of Makow for a number of hours. We passed the place where I remember two identical school buildings — one for Jewish children and one for Polish children. At this point, the current events of 1990 affected our journey, because the road leading to the schools was lined with cars and tractors for at least half a mile. Saddam Hussein had invaded Kuwait and people were waiting to fill their tanks with gasoline. I remembered a short cut, so we wove through the cars and found a path to the bridge where I used to jump into the running river and let the current pull me to the other side. Finally, we returned to the market square, which used to bustle with peddlers, merchants, and farmers from nearby villages and towns. It is on this market-square corner, on the second floor of a now-nonexistent house, that my story begins.

Part One

1939–1943

Chapter One

In the mid-1930s, before the war, violence against Jews had become increasingly widespread throughout Europe. In several countries, anti-Jewish policies had turned into laws that prohibited Jews from entering certain professions and that encouraged antisemitic violence. News and radio reports of synagogues being bombed and Jewish homes being burned became a commonplace occurrence. General antisemitic sentiments were becoming more prevalent in Poland and had begun to affect the mood in my hometown. In Warsaw, new policies prohibiting Jews from entering university were instituted and Jewish students who had already been admitted were required to stand in the back of the classrooms. All over the country there were increasing reports of random, unsolicited violence against Jewish storeowners, and anti-Jewish signs were being posted to identify Jewish businesses and encourage a Polish consumer boycott. People were filled with anxiety and concern but, in spite of these and many other telltale signs, no one correctly estimated the heinous intentions of Adolf Hitler.

On Friday, September 1, 1939, German airplanes

bombarded Warsaw and cut all lines of communication to the city. Hospitals, synagogues, and schools were destroyed. Homes were blown apart and people scattered in all directions. The threat of Hitler's war had become a reality.

Before the war broke out, my parents had discussed the possibility of leaving Makow in search of a safer place to live. However, my father, Raphael-Hirsch Azrylewicz, was a successful tailor who came from a long family-line of clothing manufacturers in the area and he resisted the idea of relocating his business and family. His business was doing particularly well, and he nurtured the hope that Britain would destroy the German forces in a few weeks and improve the escalating antisemitic climate in Poland.

My father spent most of his time working in his factory located in the front part of our house. He had at least four employees who worked with him on a full-time basis, a number of sewing machines, and a separate area where he cut and pressed material. There was also a formal showroom where he displayed his finished products and received customers for individual fittings and orders. He was a very accomplished tailor and well known throughout the region for his custom-made fur coats and suits. In fact, many wealthy German clients would travel great distances from Prussia specifically to buy his clothing.

By the time war broke out in 1939, my older brother, Ephraim, was nineteen years old and had already been working with my father for two years. In contrast, I was seventeen years old at the time but much less serious than my brother. I preferred spending my free time reading about politics, playing sports, or lying perched on a big pile of fabric and browsing through the latest design and fashion publications from France. I loved listening to the radio and putting on plays with neighborhood children in our backyard. I also built a kayak and loved to ride my bicycle through town. As a child, I was also very close with my younger brother, Pinchas. We used to play soccer in the fields, skate on the river in the winter, and swim in the rapids in the summer. In 1939, Pinchas was only fifteen years old and, like me, was still in school. Tzireleh, my sister, was thirteen years old and was also attending school when the war broke out. She was just a child then, the baby of the family, and adored by all of us.

Two years before the war, I had left Makow to attend a *Gymnasium* (secondary school) in Warsaw, which specialized in training teachers in Jewish subjects. At the time, there was no secondary school in my small town, and my acceptance to this program was a source of great pride for both me and my family. I had to pass difficult entrance exams in order to be accepted, and not every local family could afford the tuition. At the teacher's institute, we were not only taught subjects like math and science but also Hebrew language and literature. We were also trained in introductory paramilitary skills, and, for certain drills, we were required to wear special uniforms with shiny buttons. My year in Warsaw was very formative because it was the first time that I lived away from home and, although I had four or five close friends, I remember feeling quite homesick most of the time. In spite of these lonely feelings, I also enjoyed exploring the big city. I had my first experience of riding a trolley car, saw my first live theatrical production, and mingled for the first time with Polish children on the soccer field. Although antisemitism was becoming more pervasive, I was fortunate and had never personally experienced any violence.

The year I lived away from home, I was also exposed to ideas that started to influence my view of the world. In elementary school I had a wonderful teacher, Wesolek, who taught me about history and encouraged me to draw Polish and Jewish heroes. In school in Warsaw, I read books by Victor Hugo and Upton Sinclair. For the first time, I developed the language to discuss ideas like universal justice and equality for all. My parents perceived my new ideas as quite "leftist," but they always encouraged me to learn more — particularly my mother, who was very supportive of my desire to pursue a secondary education. On one visit home that year, I recall that my father was having a dispute with an employee and I sided with the employee and even encouraged him to start a union! One year later, a local secondary school opened in town so I returned to Makow to be near my family. I was happy to be back, but, as I had already tasted the freedoms of a big city, I dreamed of the day that I would move away from Poland and see the rest of the world.

The pre-war climate in 1938 and 1939 cast a shadow over our lives, but we still continued with our normal routine. I built a radio with a crystal inside and earphones so I could listen to news and music late at night. I loved discussing politics and my new theories on social justice. I was also becoming acutely aware of the danger the impending war would have for the Jewish people. In contrast, my father maintained an optimistic outlook and believed that the Allies would stop the Nazis before they could do any real harm. He simply could not believe that his loyal German clientele would also be responsible for his murder. He also still remembered World War I, when the Germans were less hostile to the Jews than the Russian Cossacks. But, while my father believed we were safe in Poland, my mother was terribly concerned about the impending war. She frequently voiced her desire to move to Palestine and insisted that the Jewish people needed a land of their own in order to be safe from the likes of Adolf Hitler.

With the outbreak of war on September 1, it became increasingly obvious that Pinchas and I were in danger of being forcibly taken to build fortifications for the Polish army or of being captured by the Germans for some other unknown purpose. One month earlier, Ephraim had been drafted into the Polish army to build roads and prepare for war, and we were still anxiously waiting for his return. On the evening of September 3, 1939, we gathered around the dining-room table and my parents decided that Pinchas and I should flee from Makow. We knew that Reuven Lesman, my friend and neighbor, and Hanoch Kirshenbaum, my uncle through marriage, were planning to leave Makow the following morning. Our plan was to travel with them in an easterly direction and then turn southward toward Palestine. Our main goal was to keep running away from the advancing Nazi forces. If we were to be separated at any time, we were instructed to head in the direction of Palestine and make contact whenever possible.

My father went into his workshop and sewed special knapsacks with secret compartments in the lining where we could hide our money and valuables. My mother packed food, homemade jams, and clothing. I will never forget the anticipation and excitement I felt that late night. I was seventeen years old, and it seemed like I was embarking on a thrilling adventure. I wanted to go and I do not remember feeling scared. I had been waiting for an opportunity to leave the small backwater town of Makow and was being offered my first opportunity to get out in the world. But, while I was excited at the prospect of leaving, my mother was terribly upset. Now that I am a parent myself, I can imagine the grief and fear my parents must have felt, and I admire their courage in foreseeing that Pinchas and I would be safer away from Makow. How terrible it must have been for them to admit that we could no longer consider our home a safe place if we hoped to survive the war.

Early on the morning of September 4, we gathered in the living room and then left the house to meet the other two men. We stood at the edge of town and bade each other farewell. None of us knew when we would see each other again, but we were all hopeful that it would be only a short time before we were reunited.

Chapter Two

Our plan was to travel eastward through Poland and then southward to Romania, and from there we hoped to make our way to Palestine. We set out on foot and stopped in Pultusk where we slept with many other refugees in an old school building. Early the next morning, we pushed forward to the next town of Wyszkow, but we left in such a rush that I grabbed two boots of the right size but of different colors — one black and one brown. They both fit, so when I finally noticed that my feet did not match, it was far too late to turn back.

It is the leg of our journey between Pultusk and Wyszkow that has stayed ingrained in my memory as my true awakening to the reality of war. Until that time, I considered walking covertly through the day and night a novelty. Although we encountered hundreds of other refugees on our travels and heard the sounds of gunfire throughout the day, we had not yet been directly confronted with the horrors of war. On the stretch from Pultusk to Wyszkow, I saw my first casualties. The victims were not people, but cows and horses that had been sprayed with bullets from German air bombers. These images of innocent animals hit by flying shrapnel and bombs made a lasting impression on me. In 1990, I must have told my daughters the story of these images at least four or five times on the drive from Makow to Pultusk and Wyszkow. Each time I forgot that I had already mentioned the impact and heartbreak I had felt when I saw those dying animals. It was also my first realization that I should probably fear for my own life.

The town of Wyszkow is situated at the intersection where the Bug and Liwiec waterways join together and flow into the main artery of the Vistula River. This junction was of important strategic value to the Polish and German forces because it provided access to major industries and commerce in Warsaw. Fifty years later, when we drove through Wyszkow, I asked our driver to stop at the modern bridge that had replaced the one I had crossed with Pinchas and the other men. My daughters and I got out of the car and walked to the bottom of the river bank where the land was covered with trees and overgrown grass. The terrain was not that different from the way it was when we lay down on this bank, exhausted and scared, and realized that we had to cross the bridge before it was demolished by the advancing German forces.

On September 5, 1939, my companions and I lay down in the brush overlooking the bridge and river. Sirens sounded every few minutes but, between each bombardment from above, there was absolute calmness. The moments between attacks were serene, when all movement and life seemed suspended. After each round of gunfire, we were lulled by this spreading silence into a deep and deadly sleep — only to be brutally awakened moments later by another thundering attack from above. Pinchas had fallen asleep after one of these attacks with his arms wrapped around a tree. When the next explosion came, he was in such a deep slumber that he did not wake up, and I will never forget the sight of my fifteen-year-old brother sleeping through the assault, hugging the tree closer to his chest and crying "*Oh, Mammeleh! Mammeleh.*"

We lay in that brush all afternoon until the bombing stopped. At dusk, we finally crossed the bridge and pushed on to the next town of Wegrow. By the early evening, we were exhausted and decided that we simply could not walk any further. We decided to sleep by the side of the road and, as we lay down, too exhausted to move, we saw people riding toward us with a wagon. Jewish families from Wegrow had heard that an influx of refugees was arriving from the west. They picked us up and brought us to their homes. They fed us, gave us their beds, and showed us such tremendous kindness that I have never forgotten them.

On the morning of the third full day of our journey, we woke up in Wegrow, washed ourselves in the river, and moved forward to our next, unknown, easterly destination. That morning, the sounds of German bomber planes seemed closer than before. After traveling a few kilometers,

I turned to look back at the town where we had met such generosity. But in its place I saw a skyline lit with fire. Wegrow had been attacked from the air and had been set ablaze. Stunned, my companions and I realized that we would never have a chance to repay their kindness. Steadying ourselves, we picked up our pace and kept moving. We knew we were only one small step ahead of the advancing Nazi troops.

David's parents: Sara Chaya and Rafael Hirsch

David (sitting), elder brother Ephraim (standing), mother Sara Chaya,
younger brother Pinchas (sitting on table) and father Rafael Hirsch

Standing (from left to right): Uncle Azriel, Fremet (wife of Uncle Samuel Joseph), Uncle Samuel Joseph and Rafael Hirsch. Sitting grandparents Ztireleh and Mordechai Azrylewicz

Top row (standing second from right): father Rafael Hirsch. Bottom row (second from left): mother Sara Chaya holding baby David and toddler Ephraim, (sitting, bottom right) Aunt Esther

Grandmother Rachel with mother Sara Chaya and little sister, Esther (David's aunt)

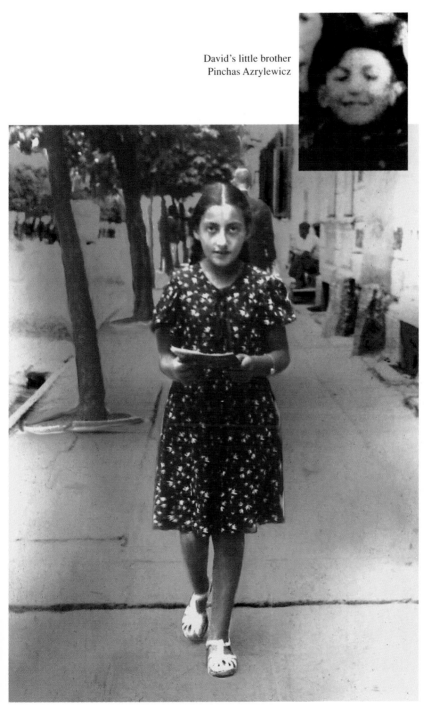

David's little brother
Pinchas Azrylewicz

David's little sister Tzireleh Azrylewicz

Mother, Sara Chaya

Family picture taken during David's mother's visit to England for her niece's wedding. Standing (second from left): mother Sara Chaya (fourth from left) Aunt Esther

David's brother Ephraim and cousin Henya, in Makow

A group of students at the Makow School with beloved teacher, Wesolek (circled, center). David (circled third from the right), Pinchas, David's younger brother (circled, center-left)

David and a friend from the seminary in Warsaw, wearing student uniforms

David with other students in Warsaw

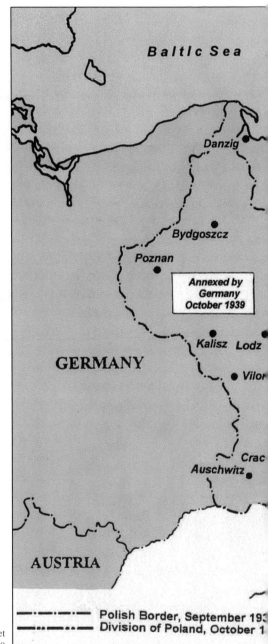

Escape route at the onset
of the War, Sept. 1939

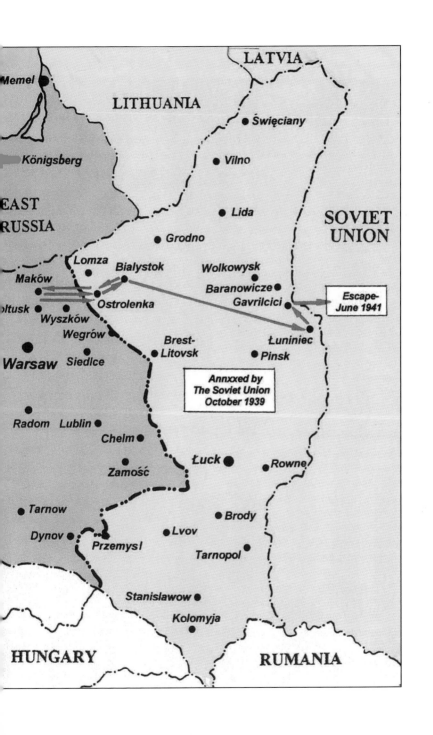

Escape from Makow to Maoz Chaim

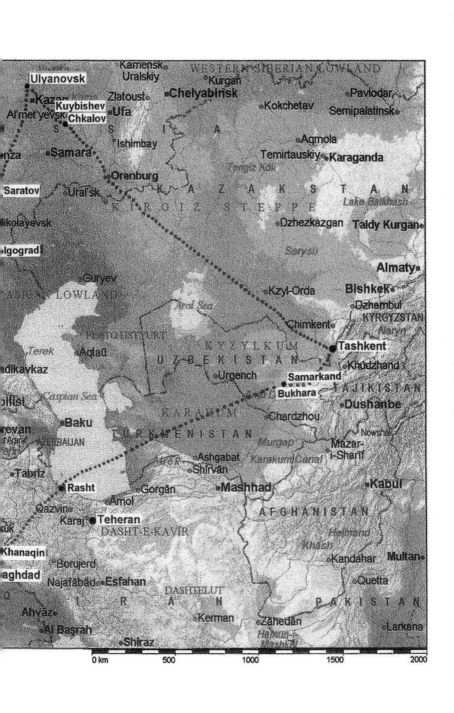

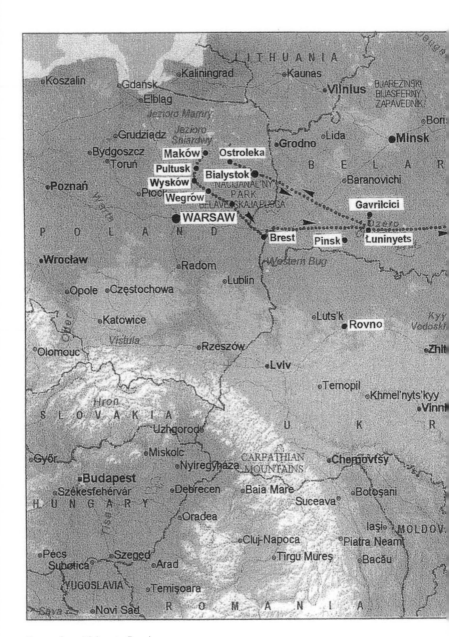

Escape from Makow to Russia

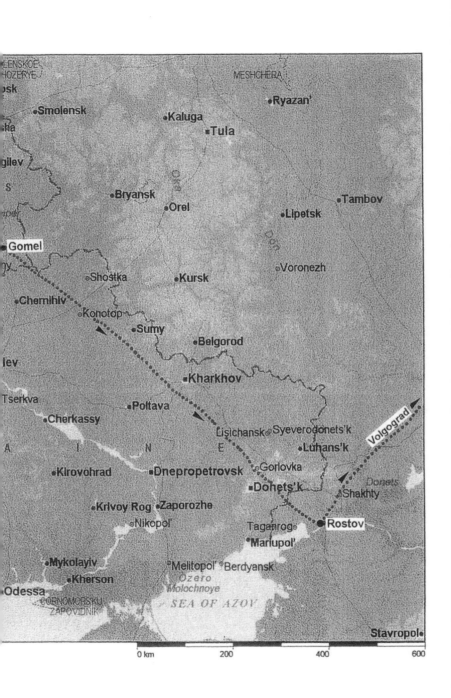

Chapter Three

My daughters and I drove through the small towns I had passed on foot during the first days of the war. The next destination on our itinerary was the concentration camp Treblinka, followed by Auschwitz and Birkenau. My mother and sister were killed in Birkenau, and my father in Auschwitz. I had never been to either camp before and I was feeling very agitated and upset about our scheduled visit. Many people I know returned to these camps after the war to mourn or to say *Kaddish* (the "Mourner's Prayer") for their murdered family members — but I never did. Ten years ago, I had visited Treblinka but I did not mourn or say *Kaddish* there. On that trip, I did not visit Auschwitz or Birkenau so, in 1990, I had still never been face-to-face with the actual place where my parents and sister were killed.

We drove to Treblinka first and it was obvious from our stilted and cautious conversation that we were all very anxious. On our way to the camp, we passed the tracks that had brought trainloads of Jewish victims to their deaths, and we saw the sign that indicated that they had arrived in Treblinka. Our Polish driver walked to the entrance with us, and when we stopped to read the factual synopses of the atrocities committed there, the driver was astonished by what he read. In school, he had been taught that Treblinka had been a work camp for criminals, and not an extermination camp for Jews. We walked through the rest of the camp without him and, while it was emotional for me to see the memorial at Treblinka, I was mentally preparing myself for our next stop: Auschwitz.

After the war, books were written to memorialize each of the small towns in Poland as a way of preserving the people and customs that had been obliterated by the Germans. In the commemorative book on Makow, the writer, Mordechai Ciechanover, remembers the day the Nazis gathered Jewish families together and started transporting them to concentration camps.

It was November 18, 1942. German soldiers chased people out of their homes and everyone was rounded up in the market square. Old people, women, and children were mercilessly beaten. Those too sick to walk were carried out in chairs. People huddled together and were forced to witness the ferocious beatings and murders of close friends, neighbors, and relatives. Ciechanover reports that after witnessing a bloody beating, my father stepped forward from the line and suddenly behaved as if he had lost his mind. He started dancing, clapping his hands, and telling everyone: "*Frailich! Leibedik! Frailich!*" ("Be happy! Be lively! Be happy!") Then he started singing:

34

A yid zu zein is tayer. A yid zu zein is gut.
Ich dank dir Gottenyu, vail ich bin a yid...

To be a Jew is dear, to be a Jew is good.
I thank you my God, that I am a Jew.

He carried on like this for a few moments and then returned to his place in line. Everyone was sure he would be shot instantly. Ciechanover ran up to him and yelled, "Are you crazy? What are you doing?" He remembers that my father replied: "I am acting this way intentionally. I have a clear mind. I already know what is going to happen... and I want them to shoot me. Why should we stand by here and witness this terrible suffering?"

From Makow everyone was sent to live in a ghetto in the bigger town of Mlawa and, within a few weeks, the trains came and took them to Auschwitz.

I had avoided my confrontation with Auschwitz for many years. Even the prospect of going there made me nervous and uncomfortable. When we arrived at the camp, we walked through the tourist reception building and were ushered into a movie room to see a biased Red Army documentary on the liberation of Auschwitz, which focused on the unjust imprisonment of Russian soldiers, and which minimized the systematic extermination of the Jewish people. Before I walked through the door to see the movie, however, I suddenly realized that I was hungry. We had been so anxious about our agenda that morning that none of us had eaten. So I went to the cafeteria and ordered a hearty lunch. Fortified by my meal, I felt ready to go inside.

By coincidence, the movie room was filled with Native Americans dressed in full traditional costume. They were visiting Auschwitz as an act of solidarity in the universal fight against genocide and discrimination against any minority group. When the documentary was over I felt very sad and heavy-hearted that, even after all these years, there was still an obvious attempt to revise the terrible history associated with this death-camp. The Auschwitz staff then opened the doors and ushered the group of Native Americans, my daughters, and me onto the grassy courtyard that disguised the atrocities committed behind the gate. Over the gate we saw the sign bearing the now famous slogan "*Arbeit Macht Frei*" — "Work Brings Freedom." Still standing in front of the ironic sign is an enormous oak tree, the last thing of natural beauty most inmates saw before their deaths.

As we walked around the camp, I looked at every item and *explained* every single thing I saw out loud. My way of coming to terms with this death camp was to try to explain every item in the context of Hitler's intentions to destroy the Jewish people. I forced myself to look at all the pictures and all the exhibits. I went inside the crematorium where my father's body must have been burned and stood quietly beside my daughters. I felt devastated by the pure malice that had destroyed my family and six million other Jews. Finally, after fifty years, standing in the crematorium that may have been my father's grave, I recited the mourner's *Kaddish*.

Next door to Auschwitz is Birkenau, where over one million Jews were killed. A Jewish prisoner in Auschwitz had a small chance of survival if he or she was chosen to work, whereas a Jewish prisoner in Birkenau was sent to an almost certain death. A few years after the war, I met someone from Makow who had survived the camps. He told me that my mother and sister were murdered shortly after they arrived in Birkenau, but that my father had survived in Auschwitz for a few months. I suspect that he may have been briefly spared because of his skills as a tailor.

Birkenau is monstrous. It has not been transformed into a museum like Auschwitz, so we found ourselves looking at the original layout of the camp. There are rows upon rows of barracks where prisoners were housed before their death. The long road dividing the camp is still fenced in with barbed wire, and this road leads to the remnants of four or five crematoria where millions of people were slaughtered. While we walked around Birkenau, we saw the group of Native Americans performing a ritual of mourning next to the rubble of the crematoria. They were sitting together in a circle chanting in a low, steady manner. One man was beating a drum as they sang a beautiful and hypnotic melody. The feelings of anguish and sadness that the melody invoked in me were quite overwhelming. I was deeply moved by the emotion these non-Jewish people were expressing over the Nazi atrocities.

I, too, wanted to participate in a meaningful ritual, so I opened a small Hebrew prayer book to a random page and began reciting a prayer. I didn't care what I was reading — I simply wanted to use Hebrew words to express my sadness alongside these native people.

My daughters and I stood and embraced beside the rubble for a long time. Finally, we closed the prayer book and, without a word, we walked down the long road toward the open gates and left the camp behind.

Chapter Four

In 1939, my companions and I moved at a remarkably fast pace for six days and six nights. We traveled by night and rested by day, under trees or covered in hay and sometimes in a generous person's home along the way. During this period of running eastward, our world felt full of adventure and excitement. We were aware that we were running for our lives and yet we were surrounded by the lush Polish countryside at autumn's peak. In spite of the signs of oncoming disaster, I felt removed from the actual horrors of war. I felt lucky to be witnessing the beauty around me. The leaves were brilliant shades of red, orange, and yellow. Farmers were busily harvesting their crops. We were completely immersed in our sense of adventure, which was tainted only slightly by our knowledge that we had to keep running in order to stay ahead of the advancing Nazi troops.

Our next stop after Auschwitz and Birkenau was the city of Brest. We said goodbye to our driver and crossed the border into what was, in 1990, still the Soviet Union. The city that I had passed through as a boy had been destroyed when Germany attacked Russia in 1941, and, since then, it has been totally rebuilt. My daughters and I remained in Brest for three days, using the city as a base for day-trips to the nearby areas. Brest itself, however, felt strange and unfamiliar and did not invoke in me any major recollections of my journey in September 1939.

Pinchas, Reuven, Hanoch, and I arrived in Brest-Litovsk on a beautiful autumn day toward the end of an exhilarating week of travel. We wandered around the city and found our way to the train station, trying to decide on our next move. We knew we wanted to turn south toward Romania at some point, and we thought that Brest-Litovsk might be a good place to redirect ourselves.

We were leaning against the back wall of the train station when a young man in the uniform of a Polish army officer approached us and asked a few questions. He turned out to be a Jewish doctor, and he wanted to help. He advised us to abandon our plan of moving southward from Brest-Litovsk because the Germans themselves were on a southern course and were quickly surrounding the area. He recommended that we continue, instead, in a straight, easterly line, past the city of Pinsk, to a railway junction in Luninietz. If we still wanted to turn south, he felt it would be safer to change direction there. Since the Polish army was also moving eastward, the officer helped us get a place aboard the train being used to evacuate his unit.

The four of us sat in the back of an open freight section until we stopped in Pinsk. While the train was in the station, the officer came back to our freight car to tell us that news from the western front was very bad. The Germans were quickly gaining ground and the Nazi army would soon be in the vicinity. He could not help us any longer, and we would have to continue on our own. We disembarked and learned that another train was scheduled to depart from Pinsk to Luninietz. We bought tickets and settled into a comfortable passenger section.

The first hour of the journey was uneventful. After a few hours, however, we heard German bomber planes hovering overhead. Suddenly, without warning, our train was riddled with bullets. The sound was like thunder in the sky. The train screeched to a halt, and all the passengers ran for cover in a deep ditch beside the tracks. Looking around, I was relieved to see that no one in my compartment had been hurt. When the attack subsided, we all re-boarded the train and continued onwards with our journey.

The bomber planes attacked our train three times. Each time the train stopped, and each time we ran for cover in the ditches outside. By the fourth air attack, Pinchas and I had become strangely accustomed to the buzzing and rattle of the bullets overhead. The next time we heard a bomber plane approaching, we brazenly decided to remain inside the train rather than seek refuge in the ditch. In the last attack, indeed, some people who ran outside were wounded while we remained safe inside the train — so it seemed like our nonchalance paid off.

For the fourth attack, the train came to a full stop, but we remained comfortably seated inside. This time, we heard the planes descend lower than previously, so low, in fact, that they nearly skimmed the roof of our compartment. In a panic, we hid under the benches, crouching beneath the seats. In order to make room, I placed my arm around the man huddled next to me. Before I could actually feel anything, suddenly I realized I had been shot. A bullet had gone through the roof of the train, through my forearm, and into the man beneath my arm. I had two bleeding holes on either side of my arm and the young man was dead.

Our train was no longer under attack, but I was in shock, and it was unclear how long I would have to wait before receiving medical attention. My bone was shattered, and my clothes were soaked with blood. A Polish soldier came to assist me with some bandages but he didn't have any iodine to clean the wound. He explained that the acid in my urine would help prevent infection so I urinated on my arm, and passed out.

When we arrived in Luninietz, we were again greeted by Jewish families waiting to help refugees in need of shelter. We were fortunate to meet the Becker family who lived in a small house warmed by a free-standing oven in the middle of the kitchen. The Beckers were wonderful people who instantly made us feel at home. I lay delirious in their living area while the other boys relayed the story of the bomber attacks on our train. I was very sick and needed immediate medical attention but the closest hospital was south of Luninietz in Rovno. The next morning Pinchas escorted me by train to Rovno, and we said goodbye to Reuven, Hanoch, and the Beckers. The Beckers gave us an open invitation to return to their home if we needed a place to stay before the next leg of our journey.

The train ride from Luninietz to Rovno was an unbearable experience of helplessness. Once again our train was attacked from above by German bomber planes. At each attack, the train stopped to allow the passengers to run for cover in the ditches alongside the tracks. I insisted that Pinchas run outside, but I remained alone in the train, stretched across the length of a bench, too weak to move. There was no way I could predict where the bullets would fall or if I would become their target. I was unprotected and absolutely terrified.

Thankfully, we arrived in Rovno safely and I was taken to a makeshift hospital in a converted elementary school. There was a shortage of beds, so I was placed on a cot in the hallway and was more or less ignored by the staff. After the first uncomfortable night, however, I awoke to the sight of a Russian nurse tending my wound. It was September 17, 1939. Germany and Russia had just divided Poland into the German-western side and the Russian-eastern side pursuant to the Molotov-Ribbentrop Pact. Rovno was on the eastern side, so thousands of Russian soldiers and medical staff suddenly flooded the city. The Russian nurse treated my shattered bone by covering the open bullet holes with a plaster cast and I was told to return to Rovno in three weeks. To this day, I remember the removal of the cast as a very painful experience because the plaster had been placed directly on my skin and was completely stuck to the open wound and the hair around it.

My injury meant that we had to reassess our plan. Pinchas and I traveled back to Luninietz to stay with the Beckers during my recuperation. The Beckers told us that Reuven and Hanoch had moved to Bialystok upon learning that many families from Makow had escaped the German occupation by relocating to the Russian-occupied zones of Poland. We also heard that our brother, Ephraim, had finally returned home after completing his army detail in late September and that only a few days after his return, news that I had been wounded reached my family. Ephraim left Makow in search of me and my brother and, hopefully, to find a safer place to live. On his journey, he also saw that life was better for Jews in Bialystok and he decided to stay there with his girlfriend, Miriam.

Since all reports indicated that the situation was relatively comfortable under the Russians, and Pinchas and I could even attend school, the thought of moving closer to our family was very appealing. At that point in our journey, we were no longer sure we could make it to a southern transit point like Romania. Due to my injury, we knew our mother would be frantic with worry. Based on these factors, we decided to travel to Bialystok and looked forward to finding fellow refugee relatives and friends. We also hoped that I would be able to find a way home in order to show our mother that I was still alive.

Chapter Five

After the German and Russian partition of Poland, Germany's new borders extended eastward, which increased the number of Jews living under the Third Reich. On October 6, 1939, Hitler declared that strict measures were needed to "adapt and regulate" the Jewish problem. Thousands of Jews were stripped of their possessions, driven out of their homes and forced to live in ghettos. One of the ways for the Jews of Poland to escape this persecution was to find refuge in the Russian-occupied territories. Hundreds and thousands of Jews fled from the German-occupied side of Poland and clustered in towns east of the new borders in cities like Bialystok. Some families believed that women and children would be safe under the German occupation, so they split up. Other families refused to move at all.

When Ephraim arrived in Bialystok, he set up a temporary home close to our Uncle Shmuel Yosef and his children Abie, Henya, Hella, and Tzireleh. And, even though our cousins the Piankas and the Rzepkas also moved to Bialystok, my parents refused to leave their home.

My year in Bialystok was marked by three separate journeys from the Russian-occupied side of Poland to the German-occupied side. My first journey home was in October 1939, in order to assure my mother that I was still alive and well. At that time, the borders between the Soviet and German sides were not well patrolled. It was not terribly difficult to travel from Bialystok, within Soviet territory, to the new German-Russian border located in the small town of Ostrolenka. I planned to cross into the western part of the country in Ostrolenka and then hitch a ride to the outskirts of Makow. Farmers who lived on the fringes of these new borders had created a thriving business for themselves transporting refugees from one side to the other. I had no trouble finding a farmer willing to drive me to the edge of Makow.

Although I was nervous, this first journey across the border was fairly uneventful. The driver dropped me off at the outskirts of Makow to avoid attracting the attention of patrolling German troops. I sat in the bushes next to the bridge leading into town and watched the streets for nearly five hours. I was shocked to see that my little town had been completely overtaken by Nazi soldiers. It seemed so different from when I left that my boyish homecoming expectations were painfully shattered.

I avoided passersby and waited for darkness. My plan was to cross the market square a few minutes before curfew and pretend to be rushing home. I avoided contact with everyone because I had no idea who could be trusted. I had not yet personally witnessed the Nazis' random brutality against Jewish boys chosen for public ridicule, but I had heard frightening stories of violence and death. Thousands of people were killed during those early days of the German occupation, but I was less concerned about contact with German soldiers than I was about being seen by my Polish neighbors. I knew a German would not be able to identify me as a Jewish boy, but my neighbors could recognize me — and betray me.

When darkness finally fell, the streets rapidly emptied. I had only a few moments to walk home protected by the rush of people hurriedly passing through town. I left my hiding place, crossed the familiar bridge, and walked across the market square with premeditated nonchalance. I was sure my fear was transparent but I reached my parents' house without incident. I raced around the house to the backyard, ran up the stairs, and knocked softly on the door. No one answered. I knocked again. I could hear my parents shuffling around inside. In retrospect, I realize that my parents must have been afraid to answer the door but at the time, I was desperate for them to let me inside. I knocked much harder the third time and cried frantically, "Mama, Papa, it's me, Szyja-David! Open the door!" Finally, I heard my mother rush to the door. She hesitated, pulled the latch and, at long last, the door swung open.

The excitement of my arrival gradually subsided and I found myself sitting around the dining-room table with my parents in their usual positions. My father was at the head of the table, sitting back in his chair with a serious and preoccupied look on his face. My mother was bustling around the table, making tea and serving my favorite homemade raspberry jam on biscuits. For a brief moment, it felt as though nothing had changed — except that we were discussing the unusual events of my last few weeks. I told them that on my adventures through the towns of Wegrow, Brest, and Luninietz, I had experienced more kindness and more terror than ever before in my seventeen years. I told them about the casualties of war and the poignant, brutal images of livestock dropping dead from bullets raining from the sky. I told them how Pinchas and I had slept outside under the stars and how I was shot while crouching under a bench on the train. I explained that, since the incident on the train, I was constantly aware of the sounds of German soldiers — even right at that moment, while sitting in the safety of the family home. I was desperate to convince my parents to find some way to get out of German-occupied Poland. I no longer believed the war would end quickly and I felt concerned about their safety for as long as they remained in Makow under the Nazi occupation.

Throughout my childhood, my mother had always defined herself as a Zionist. She frequently spoke to friends and family about the need for a Jewish state and of her willingness to give up her material comforts to move to Palestine. On that first evening home, we spoke of her Zionist convictions and of my family's lost opportunity to move to Palestine before the outbreak of the war. My father remained convinced, however, that the "phase" of hardship they were now experiencing would soon end. His business was still thriving and his customers treated him well. He simply could not believe that his life was in danger from the Germans.

I stayed home for three restful days, but it soon became painfully obvious that I could not remain in Makow. It was only a matter of time before someone discovered my presence and I would be taken away — or killed on the spot. Stories of Nazi cruelty were circulating wildly. Both Jewish and non-Jewish Polish civilians were being shot at random, but the most common targets were young men. There were also rumors that all Jewish men were being taken to forced-labor camps. I knew I had to return to my refuge in Bialystok as quickly as possible.

Before I left, however, I contacted my girlfriend Gucia Pianka. Gucia and I were actually distant relatives and we had grown up together in Makow. We had played together since we were young children, and, in the few months before I left Makow, we had started an adolescent romance filled with promises and confessions of love. During those few days at my parents' house, Gucia visited often. On the third day of my return visit, an hour before I was scheduled to leave for Bialystok, I felt compelled to sneak out of my parents' house and walk the short distance to Gucia's home. I was on a mission to convince her parents that Gucia would be safer in Bialystok with me than if she remained in Makow with them.

Gucia's father came to the door and greeted me warmly. When I informed him of the purpose of my visit, however, he dismissed my attempt as a mere childish gesture. He did not, for even a moment, consider letting Gucia come to live in Bialystok. I was terribly disappointed but when I left Makow that night, I said goodbye to Gucia in the hope that we would soon be reunited. Many years later, I learned that Gucia, my first love, shared the fate of millions of Jewish victims and perished with the rest of her family in one of the Nazi concentration camps.

My two brothers, Miriam and I spent the end of 1939 and the winter and spring of 1940 in the relative calm of Russian-occupied Bialystok. We were comparatively well off, because my parents had given Ephraim money and valuables when he left Makow so, although we had been uprooted, we maintained a sense of stability in our "makeshift" family. Miriam lived with us, kept house, and took care of us. Ephraim worked, and Pinchas and I were enrolled in the local school in an attempt to complete our secondary educations.

Actually, I recall this period of my life as a time when I genuinely enjoyed my studies. Life in Russia felt broader and more interesting than the stifling atmosphere of Poland. I learned to speak Russian, and I continued to develop my theories of social justice. Many of those high-school days were spent in long conversations with fellow students about how to achieve a fair society where all people would be treated as equals. I was attracted to art and music, and I was thrilled because I had the opportunity to hear a live symphony orchestra perform for the very first time. Bialystok provided an environment that opened new worlds of experience to me so, in spite of the worsening political climate, I actually recall that period of living and learning in Bialystok as a free and happy time.

Notwithstanding my personal feeling of contentment, the political situation continued to make the refugee community uneasy. While there was still peace in the Soviet territories to the east, there was an ongoing, devastating war continuing in the west. News reports from the western front described overwhelming victories for the Nazi army from France to the Netherlands. In the face of the obvious German military success, the conventional wisdom of the day was still to "wait and see." We held fast to our belief that it would only be a matter of time before the Allies would conquer Hitler and everything would return to normal.

My second journey to Makow was with my cousin Henya in December 1939. The winter months were very cold and we needed more supplies. By this time, it was a little more difficult to travel to the border in Ostrolenka, but we made our way west of Bialystok and found a farmer who was willing to drive us to Makow. Now, due to the uncertain outcome of the war and the future value of currencies, the farmer was less interested in our zlotys and more interested in our promises of winter supplies. He drove us to Makow and into the yard of my parents' house in exchange for winter coats and materials from my father's factory. This time Henya and I saw our families for only a few brief moments. In less than twenty-four hours, we collected supplies, loaded the wagon and began our return trip to the Soviet side of Poland.

Well into the night, our driver brought us to a village near the Russian border. He convinced us that border security had tightened considerably since our last trip and that we would be safer spending the night at his friend's stable instead of trying to cross the border at night. When we arrived at the stable, we were greeted by his Polish friends who gave us blankets. Surrounded by efforts to make us comfortable and secure, Henya and I left our parcels in the wagon covered with hay and went to sleep in a warm, dry barn.

I awoke suddenly because someone was shaking me. I focused my sleepy eyes just as the driver of the wagon punched me in the face. He and his friends started beating Henya and me with sticks. We ran out of the barn and tried to get to the wagon to salvage our winter parcels, but everything was gone. I will never forget the anger and bitterness I felt that night as I realized we had been fooled by the Polish villagers who had pretended to be our friends. At that time some German border guards had developed a reputation for robbing refugees when they were captured at the border, so these Poles had decided to raid our supplies and steal everything of value before turning us over to them. The men surrounded Henya and me and waited for the German soldiers to come get us.

Fortunately for us, the border guards we encountered were older men who had been drafted and stationed in non-combat positions. These men were not interested in us and released us after a short time. Henya and I began walking through the dense woods that separated west from east. These woods — the same woods that I had once loved — now confused and scared me. The immensity of the trees and the overpowering natural beauty of the deep forest completely disoriented me. I lost all sense of direction and time, but I am sure we walked for many hours. I think we must have walked in circles, covering the same ground over and over again, because I simply could not get my bearings. We had no idea where we were, how long we had been walking, or how we would find our way out of the forest. Finally, we saw a vehicle at the edge of the woods and surfaced, by sheer luck, on the Russian side of the border. We found our way back to Bialystok — empty-handed.

My third journey to the German-Russian border that year was to escort my mother back to Makow after she bravely crossed over to the Russian side to visit my brothers and me. It was mid-February 1940, and the winter had been very cold and bitter. The news reports indicated that the Russians and Germans were planning to shut all borders and prohibit any further access to the German-occupied zones of Poland and, since my mother had not seen Pinchas since we had left Makow on September 4, 1939, she insisted on coming to visit us.

My brothers and I met my mother at the border, and we stayed together in the city of Ostrolenka for a few days. She brought many parcels of food, warm clothing, and money. When it was time for her to return to Makow, I volunteered to escort her because, due to my two previous visits, I was the most experienced for the task. We made our way to the now familiar border crossing but, this time, I was not surprised when two German guards took us in for questioning. My mother and I had agreed in advance that if we were stopped, we would pretend that we were simply returning to the Soviet side of the border. Luckily, these German soldiers were as apathetic as those I had encountered previously, and we were held for no more than an hour before they let us go. The wagon I had arranged for my mother was still waiting. I watched as she climbed on board and as the driver shook the horses' reins. Then I returned to Ostrolenka to pick up my brothers and to start our return trip to Bialystok. Less than one month from that time, the border was completely shut, and all covert visits stopped. I never saw my mother again.

Chapter Six

In late April 1940, the school year in Bialystok was almost over and winter was showing its first signs of resignation. Many of the refugees were becoming weary and discouraged from the seemingly endless war. By this time Denmark and Norway had succumbed to the Nazi invasion and Hitler was heading toward Holland, Belgium, and Luxembourg. In spite of all of the terrible news, we received letters from my parents that indicated that life under the Nazi occupation was not too bad. People continued to live in their homes and sleep in their own beds. Over time, they had adjusted to the curfew and the new rhythm of life in the small town.

That spring the Soviets implemented a plan requiring all refugees to register their nationalities with the authorities and to indicate whether or not they were willing to accept Soviet residency-status or, instead, to return to their homes in the German-occupied part of Poland. At that time, after almost a year of living in Bialystok, many refugees were tired of being separated from their families and gladly accepted the opportunity to return home. Those people who decided to stay on the Russian-occupied side received a Soviet passport that identified them as Poles, and they were required to move at least 200 kilometers away from the new borders.

Most of my relatives, including my brothers, chose to register to go back to the German-occupied side of Poland. People believed that the effects of the war on their lives could not get much worse, and they were encouraged by their families who seemed to be managing fairly well at home. But a few people, like myself, decided to remain in Russia. The trepidation at striking out on my own was outweighed by my exciting educational experiences in Bialystok and my eagerness to leave small-town life in Makow. It seemed only natural for me to choose to stay in the Soviet-occupied zones since I was enjoying my comparative freedom and I wanted to continue studying and exploring the Soviet system of social justice. I saw no future for myself in Poland and no point in returning to the Nazi occupation. I prepared to move 200 kilometers into the interior. My first plan was to visit the Beckers in Luninietz.

In the weeks that followed my departure for Luninietz, Soviet soldiers started patrolling the streets and forcibly entering people's homes. They were looking for single young men to send to Siberian labor camps, specifically those boys who had registered their intention to return to the German-occupied side of the country. Ephraim and Pinchas were outside our home in Bialystok when they were stopped by two soldiers. The men demanded that Ephraim produce his papers that showed his nationality and official status in Bialystok. Ephraim knew, however, that they were only permitted to take single men, so he dismissed their inquiries by claiming that he was married and, therefore, not eligible to be sent away. Pinchas, who was only fifteen years old at the time, was too young to be legally taken away; but because he had a rather large physique, the soldiers did not believe his age. After a brief exchange, they carted both my brothers off to jail.

When Miriam heard that Ephraim and Pinchas were being held in prison and would be sent away to labor camps, she went to the police station and demanded that they free her "husband." When Ephraim and Miriam registered their respective intentions to return to the German-occupied side of Poland, they each registered on the "single" list, because they were not, in fact, actually married. At the police station, however, Miriam insisted that they had registered on that list in error because, in the Soviet Union, a wife was not required to take her husband's last name. She demanded that they release Ephraim and, after much cajoling, they agreed to release him — but not Pinchas. No one expected them to keep Pinchas since he was only fifteen years old, but because he was so tall and muscular the authorities simply would not release him once they had him in captivity.

Ephraim knew that if he was found walking in the streets of Bialystok again he was in danger of being taken to jail so, the next day, Miriam returned to the police station for Pinchas by herself. Upon her arrival at the police station, the guard told her that all the prisoners had already been sent away. No one has ever seen or heard from Pinchas since that time.

Soon thereafter, all of the Jewish refugee families living in Bialystok, including my uncle and cousins who had registered their desire to return to the German-occupied part of the country, were awakened in the middle of the night and taken to the train station. It was obvious that they were not being sent to the German-occupied zone, but that they were being transported to work camps in Siberia. In a panic, Ephraim and Miriam, who were not on the list of "families" being rounded up, joined the group in an attempt to stay close to our Uncle Shmuel Yosef and cousins. At the train station, however, everyone was split into groups, and they were separated. Ephraim realized that he had no money, so he caught our uncle's eye and motioned to his empty wallet. Uncle Shmuel Yosef tossed him some money just before the trains came and the groups were taken in separate directions.

Ironically, the group of refugees that was sent to work settlements was the largest group of Polish Jews to survive the war because the settlements in Siberia were not extermination camps. The living conditions were brutal but there was no instituted plan of systematic extermination. If you could work, you could survive. Through this horrific Soviet deception, many Jews, including Ephraim, Miriam, and my cousins, were spared the deaths they would have met in German concentration camps.

While I was living in Luninietz, I received a letter from Ephraim informing me of Pinchas's abduction by Russian soldiers. My parents, Ephraim and I wrote many letters to the Bialystok jail but we never received any reply. Ephraim also wrote to me after he had been forcibly taken away to Siberia. He told me that, before he had been sent away, he tried to visit the jailhouse to see if Pinchas was alive but that he could not get inside.

Pinchas was not only big and muscular, but also very strong-willed. Ephraim and I have often speculated that if he was not sent to a work camp because of his age, he was probably kept in jail, where it is likely that he antagonized his jailers. In the event that he remained in prison, we suspect that he was killed when the Germans invaded the area one year later.

Chapter Seven

I stayed with the Beckers in Luninietz for a few weeks until I found a job as an accountant for a flour mill north of the city. The mill was located in Gavrilcici, a village situated in the heart of the Pripet Marshes of White Russia and close to the pre-1939 Russian borders. I would have preferred to find a job in Luninietz, closer to the Beckers, but Gavrilcici was only 50 kilometers away and the job was a secure government position that I simply could not refuse.

To get to Gavrilcici, I traveled on a narrow-line train primarily used to transport lumber and then I hitched a ride with a farmer on a horse and buggy. The ride from the train station was long and bumpy, but it was the only dirt road leading to the village. It was always in poor condition due to devastating rains and cold winter conditions. The climate was so harsh that homes were built attached to barns so farmers could feed their animals without going outside. When I arrived in Gavrilcici, I rented the back room of a large house and attempted to settle into my new life.

The flour mill was a main focal point for the

surrounding villages. Farmers gathered around and socialized while they waited for the two grinding stones operated by a steam engine to crush their grain into flour. My job was to run the daily administrative affairs of the mill for the Soviet authorities and keep all of the accounts for flour and grain transactions. The mill had originally been owned and operated by an old man of German descent but, when the Russians occupied the area, they confiscated his mill. Flour production was considered a state-owned and-operated industry. However, as the former owner was an excellent mechanic and because his technical skills were superior to anyone else in the region, the Soviets agreed to let him continue working instead of deporting him to Siberia.

I had been living in Gavrilcici for a few weeks when I became friends with the Russian administrator of the region. This administrator was a loyal and true communist who had been fortunate enough to survive Stalin's purges before he was sent to govern the small village. He was a well-educated man and an interesting source of conversation for me, since I was curious to know more about the Soviet system of government. Our friendship was solidified by his daily visits to my room, where I made regular contributions of vodka to his persistent thirst. Nevertheless, I was lonely and I enjoyed these visits. I considered the hours I spent talking with him as the ideal opportunity to discuss a few recent incidents that had disillusioned me about life in the Soviet Union. Over the previous few weeks, especially after Pinchas was taken away, I had become outraged by the Soviets' indiscriminate arrests and the existence of forced-labor camps in Siberia. I was shocked by the shortage of food throughout the country and, finally, I felt sad and disillusioned that the government was entitled to confiscate a person's hard work and business and turn it into state property.

Fifty years later, my curiosity to return to Gavrilcici was quite overwhelming, but it took two attempts in order for my daughters and me to get there. On our first attempt, we rented a car from the Intourist Office and hired a guide to direct us from the city of Brest. We expected the guide to drive us to Gavrilcici but he informed us, as we approached our rented Lada, that he didn't know how to drive. In fact, not only did this man not drive, but he also did not read maps, nor was he familiar with the region surrounding Brest or with any of the small roads leading to Gavrilcici.

For the first few hours of our journey, the guide did not utter a word until finally, after driving for at least three hours, I started to feel uncomfortable. Nothing looked familiar, and I could not believe that I had forgotten my way, even after all these years. We pulled over to the side of the two-lane road and hailed a driver in a passing bus. The driver informed us that we were at least three hours off track and that once we arrived in the general vicinity of the village, access was very difficult due to the untended roads that had eroded over the harsh winter months. We turned around and drove back to Brest.

The next day, we set out for the second time, and I was absolutely determined to find Gavrilcici. We drove along the highway and then turned onto a narrow, two-lane strip where, after many kilometers, we came upon the dirt road that I immediately recognized as the route to Gavrilcici. We bumped along this road, over enormous potholes and dirt moguls. It had been raining all day, and splashes of mud covered our windshield, so we could barely see. Finally, after what seemed like forever, I saw the sign for Gavrilcici, and we pressed on.

We stopped the car when we saw an old, inebriated farmer weaving his way around the potholes but still moving in our general direction. I asked him in Russian if he remembered the old flour mill in the village. He said that he remembered it, but that people did not depend on the mill anymore since they could now purchase flour from the nearby *kolkhoz* (collective farm). We offered him a ride if he would show us how to get to the mill, so he hopped in the car and directed us forward.

When we arrived, everything seemed identical — although somewhat smaller than I remembered. Immediately, I was struck by the smell that permeated the air. The mill had the most unforgettable smell...it emanated from the crushed wheat combined with flour and dampness. When we walked around, I found the door to the engine room that used to turn the stones and grind the flour. I opened the door and saw that a diesel had replaced the steam engine that used to be there. On this visit, however, it was the smell that made the biggest impression on me. It has been indelibly etched in my memory. If I came across it anywhere in the world, I would think only of the Gavrilcici flour mill.

In May 1940, my life in Gavrilcici developed into a routine and semblance of normalcy. I met my Russian friend to drink vodka, I worked in the mill and, in the evenings, I wrote letters to my parents in Makow, to Pinchas in the Bialystok jail, and to Ephraim in his work camp. I regularly sent Ephraim packages of honey, dried fruit, sugar, and other items that had a long shelf-life and could help him survive the harsh winter conditions in Siberia.

News from the western front was very bad, and I knew I should stay in Gavrilcici for as long as the advancing German army remained at a safe distance. During that time, I experienced many moments of intense loneliness and longing for my family. I had not seen my parents or little sister in many months. My eldest brother had been sent away to Siberia, and no one had heard from Pinchas since he had been taken to jail in Bialystok. I felt trapped in the small village surrounded by marshes. My only source of information and conversation was a drunkard, and, more importantly, the Russia that I had been so eager to explore was turning into a distant dream.

There was one spot where, I remember, I could sit quietly at the end of a long day and listen to music. The old owner lived with his daughter, son-in-law and their baby in a big house attached to the back of the mill. The son-in-law was a talented guitarist, and, often, I would pretend to work late so that I could listen to him play through an open window. I was struck by the irony of this man's situation as compared to my own. He had lost his business to the Russians and, as a result, I was the beneficiary of a secure government job. But he was left with so many things that I longed for and lacked. He was surrounded by his family and could enjoy beautiful music after a long day. During these moments, when I sat quietly near the window vicariously sharing in his joy, I envied him. I was desperately lonely and ached to be reunited with my family, surrounded by warmth and comforted by the people I loved.

Chapter Eight

I had been living in Gavrilcici for over a year when Germany invaded the Soviet Union on June 21, 1941. In only a few days, the Nazis fought their way into the Soviet mainland and seemed unstoppable. Until that time Hitler's war had been removed from the day-to-day lives of the Gavrilcici villagers. When the Germans broke their coalition pact with the Soviets, daily life in Gavrilcici and at the flour mill was immediately affected. We saw the sky light up with bombs. Cannons could be heard from the north and from the south. Our village was surrounded by fire as we watched and waited in the calm eye of the storm. We knew that because the local population was small and access was difficult due to the surrounding swamps, we were momentarily saved from the blitzkrieg. We also knew that it was only a matter of time before our temporary safe haven would be descended upon by the advancing Nazis.

In an attempt to defend themselves against the German onslaught and to prevent an influx of refugees from the surrounding areas, the Russians decided to seal all of their pre-1939 borders. As a result, all of the cities and towns in the Russian-occupied zones of Poland were trapped by the advancing Germans on one side and the defensive posture of the Russians on the other. Jews living in Russian-occupied cities like Luninietz were stuck; when the Nazis invaded the area there was no way to escape. Thousands of Jews were rounded up and slaughtered in nearby extermination camps.

On June 26, 1941, five days after Germany attacked Russia, I knew that I had to escape from Gavrilcici as quickly as possible. It had been raining for the last few days and, on that particular day, the air was heavy and suffocating. Late in the afternoon, as I was finishing my day's work, I heard something that I had never heard before in the small village — the sound of an approaching crowd. I left my post and saw hundreds of emaciated people being driven forward by ruthless Russian guards. Many of the prisoners were walking without shoes, in torn clothes, and seemed to be near death. This swarm of people was being forcibly marched through the village into a big field. My co-workers from the mill told me that it was a march of prisoners from a Soviet labor camp who had been sent to Poland to help build airfields and military fortifications. After Germany's attack, Soviet guards were ordered to drive these prisoners on foot, all the way from Brest-Litovsk, through rural villages and into the Soviet Union. Gavrilcici was the last major stop on this long march before the prisoners crossed the border into Russia and were officially out of the occupied areas of Poland.

I was horrified by what I saw, so I walked to the field to find out what these people had done to warrant this kind of terrible treatment from the Soviet authorities. I had heard rumors of mistreatment and misery in Soviet labor camps but I had never truly believed it. A few prisoners, who dared to speak to me, said they had been working in Brest-Litovsk for eighteen months and that most of them had been sentenced for political crimes or minor theft. I spoke to a disfigured woman who told me that she had been sentenced to two years of hard labor because she had stolen a spool of thread from a factory where she worked.

Appalled by what I saw, I also knew that this procession of prisoners meant that the Germans were close behind, so I immediately left the field to look for my Russian-alcoholic friend. I knew that I needed his help to escape. Perhaps he liked me — or maybe it was just because of my booze supply — but the administrator agreed to get me out of Gavrilcici before the imminent German invasion. He knew that my life was in danger because I was Jewish. I would not be protected by the local villagers once the Russians withdrew from the area, especially since my job was a direct result of the Soviet occupation. He told me that he had been approached earlier by a prison guard who needed a wagon for his sick and tired personnel. We agreed that he would give them the wagon belonging to the flour mill on condition that they take me across the border, outside of the occupied zones and inside the Soviet Union.

The sky was an ominous black. As I hitched up the mill wagon, it started to rain and the storm washed away the suffocating humidity of the past few days. I drove the wagon to the field where I met the prison guards as arranged and I crawled into the back of the wagon. Without saying good-bye to a soul, I left Gavrilcici with the marching prisoners in tow.

On our journey to the old Soviet border, we passed through a number of villages and each was completely deserted. The inhabitants of these hamlets had heard rumors of the torturous Soviet pilgrimages and had boarded up their windows until the parade of walking dead had passed. The acts of cruelty performed by the Russian prison guards was devastating to witness and served as the final blow to my illusions about the Soviet government which, obviously, did not value human life.

While hiding in the relative safety of the wagon, every few minutes I would hear a cry of agony and then a single gunshot would blast through the silence of the night. These shots increased in frequency as we traveled further. I understood that the prisoners who could no longer walk were summarily shot to death, or left wounded to die, helpless, in the swamplands.

We had been traveling all night and it was early morning when we finally crossed the border without incident. I was well hidden and the wagon full of tired Russian guards was not inspected by the border patrols. Not long after we were safely inside the Soviet border, however, we came to a small town where the guards refused to hide me any longer. They pointed to the nearest train station and left with the mill wagon.

I did my best to appear inconspicuous, but there was little I could do to hide the fact that I was a stranger in town. Only a few moments after I arrived at the station, I was approached by a policeman who started badgering me with questions. I explained that I was running from the German onslaught and that I was a government worker on my way to the state office of flour mills to collect my monthly pay. This seemed plausible since every month my paycheck was postmarked from the state office in the nearby town of Gomel (Homyl). This particular policeman, however, was intent on sending me back to Poland and there seemed to be nothing I could do to convince him otherwise.

The policeman made me sit on a bench on the station platform next to a guard who was assigned to watch me. The plan was to put me on the next train heading west toward Poland and the advancing German army. It was my good fortune however, that there were no more trains moving in a westerly direction. All the trains that passed through the station were eastbound in a last Soviet effort to evacuate Russian soldiers and army equipment from Polish soil. As I sat silently, waiting to be deported back to Poland — the equivalent of a death sentence — I gradually became aware of a pattern of passing trains. I noticed that as each train approached, it slowed down and that open freight carriers actually came to a near halt but then rapidly picked up speed again as they moved out of the station.

It seemed as if we had been sitting there for hours when my guard, who was obviously getting tired, went inside the station for a moment and left me alone. A low platform train used to transport equipment was moving into the station slowly and I seized my chance to make a dash for it.

I ran ahead of the train as fast as I could, hoping to grab a handle and hang on to the train as it picked up momentum. I calculated that if I ran far enough ahead of the first car, I may have a second chance if I missed on my first try. I ran with all my strength, determined to survive. A handle appeared alongside me, I grabbed it and then swung myself up and onto the platform. For a minute, I thought I had lost my grip but I managed to hold on. As I lay flat on my belly I heard one, two, three shots whiz past my head, but it was too late. The train picked up speed and was on its way. I was once again a free man.

After a while, I stopped trembling and lifted my head. I realized that the rain had finally stopped and it was a beautiful day. The train was passing through the rich forests of the region and once again I recognized the familiar smell of white pine trees rushing through my nostrils. I was on the move, I was alive, and I planned to stay that way.

Chapter Nine

By sheer luck, the train's first stop was Gomel where the head office of the state flour mills was located. Gomel had been circumvented by the Nazi army since it was situated in the inner belly of the country with no major strategic value. This temporary respite from the German offensive had turned the little city into a safe transit point for refugees. But, while Gomel was not in danger of immediate attack, it was still very close to the war activity, and continuous blasts of gunfire could be heard around the city. When I arrived, refugees were swarming the streets. I went straight to the mill office, which, to my surprise, was open but in complete chaos as the bureaucrats were busily preparing to evacuate. No one knew which flour mills were still in operation and which had already been captured by the Nazis, so I gave my name and official position and actually received my wages for the month!

Other refugees told me that most of the trains departing from Gomel were moving in a southerly or southeasterly direction, so I went back to the station and boarded a train that same afternoon. The train I chose did not have an actual passenger section, but it did have an empty storage compartment where passengers could sit quite comfortably. There were many people, but there was still plenty of room to stretch and rest. In my compartment I noticed a fellow named Zuckerman whom I remembered from my year in Bialystok and whom I had met again while living with the Beckers in Luninietz. He had been one of the few who were lucky enough to escape from Luninietz before the Russians shut the borders. Like me, he was traveling southeast with another Jewish boy from Minsk, in an attempt to keep ahead of the advancing Nazi army. It was comforting to meet other people in the same situation, so we traveled together in that boxcar for several days and nights. We shared our food, talked and learned about each other's families and about our respective refugee stories.

On the third morning, the train came to an abrupt stop and a guard ordered us to disembark immediately. Russian guards rounded us up into groups and assigned each group to the various *sovkhoz* (state farms) in the area. The boy from Minsk and I were assigned to a *sovkhoz* approximately 10 kilometers from the station.

Zuckerman was assigned somewhere else and we were forced to separate. One guard explained that we were in the Donbass region, not far from Rostov, in the Ukraine. We were being taken to help harvest the crops on the government-owned and-operated farm. We walked the 10 kilometers filled with apprehension and doubt, because neither of us knew anything about living on a *sovkhoz* and we had no idea what to expect.

When my new friend and I arrived at the *sovkhoz*, we were astounded by its incredible beauty. Enormous fields of wheat and pastures filled with healthy cattle lay before our eyes. As far as I could see, there were rows upon rows of wheat crops stretching into the distant horizon. It was clear that if we stayed and worked at the *sovkhoz*, we would be temporarily safe from the advancing Nazi forces and we would have enough food to survive the next few months. The *sovkhoz* administration assigned us beds in a large, comfortable room and we found boxes of work clothes ready to wear. We were overjoyed by the luck that had brought us to this wonderful paradise instead of to one of the Russian labor camps. We put down our bags and planned to stay as long as we could.

My first assignment at the *sovkhoz* was to clean the barns but, after a few days, an old blacksmith took a liking to me and requested that I be transferred to his workshop. This old man was a true craftsman, with tremendous skill in forging iron. He was extremely well respected within the *sovkhoz* community, although he was considered somewhat of an eccentric. He spoke very little, had a powerful physique, an enormous white mustache that curled at the sides of his mouth, and narrow, watchful, sparkling eyes. Since machinery and parts were difficult to obtain, this blacksmith had an essential role in the success and livelihood of the *sovkhoz*. Whenever a piece of machinery would break, he would forge a replacement piece so that the machine could be used again.

My job was to stand next to him while holding a heavy sledgehammer and pay close attention to his movements and gestures. While he hammered and molded the burning hot iron into shape, I stood by and watched his face for subtle cues. The mere blink of an eye, for example, was a silent command to hit the iron with exactly the right amount of force in a precise location. This job was very difficult because only the old smith knew exactly where, how hard, or when I should strike the iron and there were no rules that I could discern or follow. In spite of this, I truly enjoyed working with him and found it very exciting to see him create a useful tool from nothing but a sheet of metal. If I wasn't ready with my hammer when the old smith gave a sign, a whole piece would be ruined — but whenever he would glance at me with a nod of approval, I felt very proud. That summer of 1941, I became quite muscular from handling the heavy hammer and I recall feeling busy, healthy, and productive.

My time on the *sovkhoz* also conjures up memories of beautiful Ukrainian women in colorful native dresses. These women would gather around the evening bonfires and sing and dance with the *sovkhoz* workers until the wee hours of the morning. I was so enthralled by my new experience on the *sovkhoz*, there were moments when I almost forgot the war. In late summer, food was in abundance, I had a good job, and I felt content.

During those summer months, the news broadcast over the Russian radio stations was optimistic. Toward the end of the summer, however, the signs and sounds of war began drawing closer to the Donbass region. My friend from the train, his new Russian girlfriend, and I knew that we should prepare to leave the apparent safety of the *sovkhoz* and begin traveling away from the advancing German army. On the day we heard that Kiev had fallen into German hands, we knew we had to leave if we were to remain one step ahead of the Nazis. My friends and I told no one of our plans. The *sovkhoz* had been very good to us, we didn't want to panic the residents and we were uncertain about whether the authorities would try to restrain us.

We left the *sovkhoz* after midnight and started on the 10-kilometer walk back to the train station. I thought of going to the city of Baku and across the Caspian Sea toward Palestine, but it was too late. The Germans were making rapid advances on the southern front in an attempt to capture the oilfields and refineries in the area. They were trying to seize control of these refineries not only for themselves, but also to cut off supplies to the Russian army. The Russian girl wanted to travel north to find her uncle in Siberia, so I decided to join my companions in a northward direction.

Most trains were moving northeast, so we bought tickets for Stalingrad (Volgograd) and began the next leg of our journey. I noticed that the further away from the war we traveled, the less conspicuous we became and the more easily we were accepted by the people around us. That summer, the official Soviet radio stations had persisted in broadcasting optimistic reports about the war. As we started moving northward, I noticed that the reports of the war were changing. Broadcasters were no longer encouraging people to fight for a communist Russia. Instead, the reports were encouraging people to fight to defend Mother Russia from the Germans. In September 1941, patriotic songs encouraging people to defend their country blared over the airwaves. The Germans had moved into the heartland of Russia and the Ukraine. Young boys were disappearing into the army and daily life was filled with struggles common to a nation at war.

In 1990, my daughters and I took a rickety plane from Minsk to Kharkov and then transferred to a direct flight to Stalingrad. I wanted to return there to follow the exact steps of my route during the war, but I also wanted to see the vast and beautiful waters of the Volga. We found a boat tour and took a relaxing and enjoyable trip up the river. In 1941, when I took the six-day journey on the Volga, I experienced the most wonderful feelings of freedom. On this return visit, it was even more beautiful than I had remembered.

When my friends and I arrived in Stalingrad, there were radio reports that all Polish refugees who had been exiled to Siberian work camps were being released as part of a new agreement between the Russians and the Allies. When Germany and Russia divided Poland in September 1939, many Polish soldiers stationed in the Russian-occupied zones were deported to forced-labor camps. The new agreement provided for the release of these Polish soldiers and all other Polish citizens who had been exiled to Siberia. The political alliance was intended to enable these freed Polish exiles to be organized into one of two Polish armies. One army, led by General Wladyslaw Anders, would fight alongside the Allies in the west. The other army, led by General Vasilevski, would fight alongside the Russians in the east.

Upon hearing this news, I realized that if I went further north to Siberia, I would have a good chance of finding Ephraim and possibly Pinchas. My friends also wanted to continue moving in that direction, so we boarded a commercial steamer and settled down for a six-day journey heading north on the Volga. Our boat was a huge vessel loaded with people and all their possessions including livestock, chickens, and pigs. The deck was packed. It looked more like a circus ring than a steamer boat and the prevailing mood of the passengers seemed frenzied and apprehensive. In order to avoid confrontation, my friends and I climbed to the very top of the ship where we found a quiet corner away from the chaos below. We stayed perched in this sheltered corner for the entire voyage, breathing the crisp autumn air and picnicking on our remaining food. To pass the time, we sang folk songs with other passengers about the effortless movement of the ship. In stark contrast to our ship's gliding motion, we watched the shore line where desperate and tired people struggled to pull their barges along the water's edge while humming to distract themselves from the weight of their loads. We sat high aboard this ship in direct contact with the relentless wind while it buffeted back and forth against us. My skin was dried and my lungs were filled with the sweet fresh air of the open waters.

★

After my daughters and I visited Stalingrad, our trip veered away from the route I had taken during the war so that we could visit Moscow. We flew to Moscow and toured the city at a time when *perestroika* was catapulting life in the Soviet Union into complete chaos. A single package of American cigarettes could buy a lengthy cab ride or a three-course meal. After a short stay, however, we were eager to return to the West and leave the memories of the war behind us. We flew to Israel via Amsterdam and met my wife, Stephanie, in the bustling city of Tel Aviv for the Jewish New Year 5751. At this point, the present-day portion of our journey to Poland and Russia was concluded, but in the autumn of 1941, my story continues....

★

In September 1941, my friends and I spent six days traveling along the Volga River. When our boat finally docked, we found ourselves in an industrial city somewhere in the Ural mountain region. We disembarked and immediately boarded an eastbound train for Tschkaloff, a major city in Siberia. We knew that the trans-Siberian railway reached an east-west and north-south junction there. We correctly assumed that many of the freed Siberian workers would transfer at this junction and head south in search of a warmer climate. If I had any hope of finding Ephraim or Pinchas, my best chance to intercept their journey from Siberia was to wait at the train station in Tschkaloff.

When we arrived, the Tschkaloff junction was swarming with people. Train load after train load of Polish refugees were heading south. At this point, my traveling companions wanted to continue east, so we parted ways and I found a corner in the train station where I was determined to wait until I found Ephraim, Pinchas, or someone who could tell me some news about my family. I then decided to greet each and every train arriving from the north. I met several people from Makow, but I did not find Ephraim or Pinchas. I did hear from a passing traveler that Ephraim was, in fact, alive but I was unable to find out where he was or which way he was traveling.

As history later revealed, a few of the exiles released from Siberia did not travel southward through the junction at Tschkaloff but chose, instead, to stay east along the Volga River. This decision to avoid the warmer climates turned out to be very wise because the cool climate of the eastern region did not create a breeding ground for the deadly diseases of dysentery and typhoid that were pervasive in the warmer areas. It is one of nature's terrible ironies that many people traveling southward had managed to survive the living conditions in Soviet labor camps only to die from diseases transmitted through unwashed fruits in the warm southern cities. My brother, his wife Miriam, and many of my cousins were among the lucky few who avoided the southern route. However, at that time I had no idea which direction they had decided to travel, so I waited at the junction for about two weeks in the hope of finding them.

One day, as I was waiting for the next train to arrive, I

saw two young boys selling soft butter in the train station. When they left, I followed them for about 15 kilometers to a nearby *kolkhoz* where I saw them buy their butter for much less than their selling price. The next day, I woke up very early and hiked to the *kolkhoz* where I bought a huge package of butter. I walked back to the train station and sold it to passing travelers at a profit. For the next few days, I continued to purchase butter every morning and sell it at the train station for the rest of the day. By the end of the second week, trains were arriving less often, and I realized that I would have to give up the search for my brothers. In the meantime, I had replenished my dwindling funds and I bought a train ticket south to the city of Tashkent.

Chapter Ten

The train to Tashkent had passenger cars with benches and baggage racks that lined both sides of the ceiling. In an attempt to make myself comfortable, I climbed onto the baggage rack above my seat and made a little bed. I put my boots and some of my valuables under my head as a pillow, stretched out full length and fell into a deep, comfortable sleep. At one point in the evening, I was awakened by the train's sudden halt and the noise of passengers preparing to disembark and I realized that my pillow of valuables and boots was gone. I frantically searched the baggage rack but I knew that my belongings had been stolen from under my head while I was sleeping. My cherished family pictures, my diaries, and my drawings were all gone. Thankfully, I had put my money in my pockets and I still had a few photos and another pair of shoes in my pack, but I was very upset. Every item that had been stolen from under my head was very important to me — and had absolutely no value to anyone else. I suspected that they had been stolen when the train was stopped at the station so I ran out of the compartment yelling, "Thief! Thief!" I tried to get the police to help, but it was no use. No one cared that my possessions were stolen and I was forced to give up my search as the train to Tashkent got ready to leave without me.

When I arrived in Tashkent the following day, I felt very sad. Many of my cherished reminders of home were gone, I had no idea what was happening to my family in Poland, and I could not find my brothers. The only thing I knew for certain was that I had to keep moving. I was also starting to feel impatient with the war. My months of continuous running for fear of being caught by the Nazis were confirming my mother's Zionist position — the Jewish people needed a homeland in which to live freely. A Zionist future was the only way we could ever live in safety and feel secure that we would not be obliterated by the likes of Adolf Hitler.

In contrast to my dark mood, Tashkent was a bustling city filled with activity and life. It had developed into a substantial metropolis because many Russian opera and theater companies had been relocated there for the duration of the war. The people of Tashkent had also become major contributors to the war effort because a munitions factory was transplanted to the area and was being used to replenish the armaments supply. As the capital city of Uzbekistan, Tashkent had many beautiful buildings exemplifying typically Eastern architecture. I was particularly fascinated by the domes, the majestic archways, and the intricate geometric designs carefully etched into the walls of the buildings.

My travels thus far had been filled with many new

experiences, but nothing had prepared me for the shift to the Eastern styles and attitudes that I encountered in Tashkent. The city also had an air of excitement and danger; ironically, however, a significant danger at the time was the temptation to eat the enticing fruits sold on every street corner. The fruit looked so juicy and delicious that, on my very first day, I bought a bunch of grapes and greatly enjoyed eating them as I walked around the city. Soon afterward, however, I became violently sick. It was by sheer luck that I did not contract dysentery.

During those few days, I walked the streets, explored the town, and every evening I made an effort to find a clean and comfortable place to sleep. One night, I sneaked into a clean, well-preserved building and fell asleep in the doorway only to be woken up by a man in uniform screaming angrily at me. Apparently, I was sleeping in a building that belonged to the Secret Police. Needless to say, I gathered my things and left immediately!

Across the street from the Secret Police building, I noticed a pump with water trickling from its spout. Very few people were around in the early morning hours so, despite the brisk morning air, I stripped down to my waist and washed my face and torso, wet my hair, and rinsed my shirt and socks. Throughout my journey I always made a conscious effort to keep a bar of soap with me at all times. I washed and attempted to maintain my appearance whenever I could. From the moment I left Makow, I understood that my survival depended on keeping myself clean and avoiding sickness. After my bath on that morning, I walked the streets of Tashkent and learned from the local vendors that it was quite difficult to find a job in the area. Apparently, it was easier to find work in one of the smaller cities of Uzbekistan, so I decided to leave that very afternoon.

I took a train past Samarkand and decided to stop in the medium-sized city of Bukhara. I found a room with a family on my first day and immediately started my search for a job. Once again, I was impressed by the oriental architecture of the Eastern city. The room I rented was located in a traditional one-story house built around an inner courtyard. Each room of the house had a small window overlooking the patio, but the rooms themselves were kept dark and cool as protection against the intense heat.

It seemed to me that the people of Bukhara were more traditional than the people of Tashkent. Many of them wore long embroidered oriental dresses, colorful authentic Uzbeki robes, and small round *yarmulkes* with flat tops. There were many mosques in the city and even a few synagogues. These synagogues were designed and built very differently from the one I had known in Makow. The *bima* (altar) was in the center of the sanctuary instead of against the eastern wall, and everything was painted or covered in white instead of with deep colors like the synagogue at home. But I was fascinated by these differences and was happy to learn that, although the Bukharian customs and rituals were somewhat different than the ones I knew, I still felt a kinship to this Jewish community.

One day, on an exploratory trip around the city, I heard someone call my name in Yiddish. I was walking in a park and didn't know a soul in the area so I did not believe my ears. I took a cursory glance around, saw no one, and kept walking. I continued on my way and then I heard someone call my name again. This time, I took a better look around and noticed an emaciated man sitting on a bench. A dirty *foufeika* (cotton quilted robe) was draped around his body and instead of shoes, he was wearing cut pieces of rubber tied together with string. I approached him and saw that he had almost no teeth and that his face was marked with black splotches. He called to me again, but this time he said: "Szyja-David, don't you recognize me? It's David Flatau — from Makow."

The David Flatau I knew from Makow was an old family friend who had been studying engineering when the war broke out. Our families were very friendly and, as a boy, I had always admired him. The last time I had heard any news about him, he had been picked up on the streets of Bialystok and sent to the Siberian mines. The man sitting on the bench before me was near death. He had obviously been released with the other Polish exiles, and it looked as though he had been in the park for quite a while with no place to go and no strength to help himself. I was utterly shocked to see him in such a state. It made me wonder about the condition of my own family but, at that time, I still had no idea about the Nazi death camps. All I knew was that I must help David get well. I took him back to my room, and he bathed with soap and water for the first time in months. I gave him clothes, and we burned his lice-infested *foufeika* behind the house.

For the next few weeks, David recovered quietly in my room. He had a craving for fresh raw onions so I made frequent trips to the market. In retrospect, I realize that raw onions are a natural source of vitamin C, which he needed to combat the scurvy in his body. When he was healthy enough to work, we heard that someone was needed to operate a film projector in a nearby village. We were sure that, with his engineering background, David could manage a film projector, so he took the job. In fact, David worked at that same job until he left Uzbekistan years later.

David Flatau married a British woman and settled in Toronto, where he worked as a successful engineer for the Ontario Roads Department. We continued to be in close touch throughout the years, and he never seemed to forget our fateful encounter in Bukhara in 1941. Every year for *Rosh Hashanah* (the Jewish New Year), he sent my family a crate of freshly picked apples from the Niagara peninsula. My last contact with him was in March 1991, ten days before he died. He sent me a nineteenth-century edition of the book *The Works of Flavius Josephus* with beautiful illustrations and engravings of steel and wood to add to my Judaica collection.

Chapter Eleven

During my search for work in Bukhara, I met a friendly and influential Uzbekistan couple who took a liking to me. My appearance and attitudes were a novelty to them, and they enjoyed asking me about life in Western Europe. Through their connections, I found an accounting job on a *kolkhoz* located two hours from Bukhara where I enjoyed rather immediate acceptance as a member of the community. I worked very hard and, not long after I settled into my position, I was rewarded with unlimited access to a horse from the stables. In Uzbekistan, horses were valued as symbols of success, wealth, and strength. Every horse received great care and was treated with tremendous reverence, so I cherished this gift and spent many hours riding and tending to it. I also developed friendships with a number of Jewish refugees who were living on the *kolkhoz*. My closest friends were from Odessa and, as soon as we met, I felt that instant bond that persists amongst Jewish people due to our mutual Jewish backgrounds — even though they spent most of their lives in the atheistic climate of the Soviet Union.

After I had been living on the *kolkhoz* for a few months, the mother of this family from Odessa made an urgent call to my office. Their youngest daughter was very sick and in desperate need of medical attention, but the only doctor lived 20 kilometers away and they had been unable to reach him. I rushed over to their house and saw that the girl looked terribly ill. It was obvious that she needed immediate medical assistance so I went straight to the stables, saddled my horse, and galloped 20 kilometers to find the doctor. By the time I reached his office, my horse was strained and overheated, but I could not spare the time to let him rest before I started the return trip with the doctor following close behind.

When we arrived, some of the local people saw my lame, tired horse and ordered me to dismount immediately. They covered the horse with blankets and walked it slowly around in circles. I could sense a mounting tension in the atmosphere but I had no idea what I had done wrong. A nice young fellow pulled me aside and warned me that I had better leave the *kolkhoz* as soon as possible. I had caused damage to the horse, and my life was now in danger.

I could not believe that a value system existed in which a horse's life was placed at a greater premium than that of a little girl's, but the urgency in the man's voice told me to take him seriously. I left quickly, and a few days later he forwarded my few belongings with a note informing me that the little girl and the horse were fine but that, within minutes of my departure, fanatics from the *kolkhoz* had come looking for me bearing axes. My intention to save the girl was irrelevant to them. According to these people, my terrible treatment of the horse called for severe and brutal punishment.

When I returned to Bukhara, I visited my influential Uzbeki friends, expecting them to understand the events that led me to abruptly leave the *kolkhoz*. Unfortunately, they, too, valued the life of a horse over the life of a human being, and, although they took a moment to listen to my version of the events, they were not empathetic to what I perceived as a grave injustice. But while the woman of this couple showed concern for the horse, she was also concerned about some of my Western possessions. She was particularly fascinated by a pocket watch that had been given to me by my sister, Tzireleh, on the night I had left Makow in September 1939. My mother had purchased this watch on a trip to England in 1933, for her niece's wedding. My mother's brother, Nathan, celebrated the event of his daughter's marriage by sending tickets to his mother (my grandmother, Bubba Rachel) and his two sisters (my mother and my Aunt Esther) so that the whole family could gather together for the great event. It was quite extraordinary for them to travel all the way to England and, when they returned, my mother had gifts for everyone. One of her special gifts was this watch. My sister had been particularly enthralled with it because of its unusual style, which showed the inner mechanics of the clock through a transparent cover. On the night of my departure from Makow, Tzireleh had given me this watch for good luck. The Uzbeki woman was completely fixated on it — and I think she hoped I would give it to her if she helped find me another job.

A few kilometers outside of Bukhara, there was a vineyard which produced port wine and with the woman's help, I was given a job there as an accountant. I had a nice office with relative security and I could even furnish my friends with a supply of port, full of vitamins and sugar, which was helpful in combating scurvy, typhoid, and other diseases. At that time, these diseases had taken on plague-like dimensions in Bukhara. Hundreds of people were walking around the city in emaciated condition. People would fall asleep on park benches and never wake up again. Each morning, workers would go around the city pulling a platform wagon on which they collected the dead bodies that had accumulated during the night. Hundreds of nameless bodies were collected every day. It was impossible to ignore the ravages of these epidemics wherever I went.

During this time, the Polish Anders' army was recruiting men to fight alongside the Allied forces in the west. Acceptance into this army was viewed as a one-way ticket out of Russia, but most Polish men available for recruitment were in poor physical health or were still recovering from the harsh living conditions in Siberia. Polish-Jewish boys were almost always rejected by the Anders' army — not only because of their poor health, but also because Anders was a ferocious antisemite. So, although rejection was almost inevitable, it was in every Jewish boy's interest to present himself to the recruitment office and obtain official rejection papers. In theory, this rejection also prevented the Soviet authorities from claiming that a Polish boy living in Russia was shirking his military obligations, thereby protecting him from being sent away to a labor camp.

I was working in my accounting office at the vineyard when it occurred to me that I should get my official rejection from the army in order to avoid trouble in the future. It was a regular working day, but I took time off and caught a train to the recruiting office. I left my desk full of papers and intended to return to work immediately after receiving my anticipated letter of refusal. However, when I arrived at the army office and undressed for my physical, to my dismay, the doctor was delighted to see any young man in my condition. He even called the other doctors into the room and said, "Where did we find this one?!" I was nineteen years old, healthy, muscular, and well-fed. The doctor completed my physical and, as he could find no excuse to reject me, within moments I was enlisted as a soldier in the army.

I had told no one of any plan to leave Bukhara because, in my wildest dreams, I did not expect the Anders' antisemitic army recruiters to accept me. I was suddenly faced with the option of joining the Polish military forces and traveling west toward possible freedom, or staying in Bukhara and continuing the harrowing task of keeping ahead of the Nazis and, simultaneously, avoiding the Soviet work camps. I took my uniform and signed my name. In an instant I was transformed from a refugee working as a vineyard accountant into a Polish soldier and part of the Allied forces. Hopefully, that meant that I was one step closer to my goal of reaching Palestine.

In the army, I met three other Jewish boys in my unit: Izio Rosen, M. Goldberg, and Adam Fogiel. Adam and I became particularly close friends and, together, we faced the rampant antisemitism that we encountered in the army. We quickly learned to look after each other in the hostile environment. We learned to sleep in our tent, back to back, with a loaded gun between us. We were more fearful of the threat the other soldiers posed to us than of the threat of battle, and we knew that we had to withstand the antisemitism in order to successfully use the army to transport us out of Russia and toward Palestine.

Adam and I were regularly humiliated or given the most demeaning duties in our unit. It was common for an officer to order us to clean the latrines and, during morning roll call, the sergeant would often untie my boots and step on my feet, or swear at me in front of the entire regiment. One day the sergeant decided to play a game with Adam and me. He ordered us to run at his command and then, at another command, to sit on the ground and not move. After playing his little game two or three times, Adam developed a plan. The next time the sergeant ordered him to run forward, he ran so fast that the sergeant could not keep up. We both recall that incident as a great and victorious moment.

In spite of all this treatment, Adam and I persevered and were actually two of the better athletes in our unit. There were plenty of imported British rations, so we stayed in good condition, kept ourselves well-fed and healthy. In the early mornings, we would run 10 kilometers while singing marching songs. In the afternoons, we practiced engineering drills, learned to erect and dismantle special tents, and perform other maneuvers involving roads and bridges. We would frequently perform our duties better than the others, but this only incited the people in command to humiliate us more. We were also obviously better educated than most of the other boys. In fact, Adam was fluent in English and Russian, and quickly became the official translator for army business.

Our base camp was very close to a river, which turned red from the sediment that accumulated in the mountain runoff. On some nights, Adam and I would lie near this river under the open skies and spend hours talking about our futures. We discussed our childhoods, our plans, our wartime experiences, the future of the Jews, and our hopes that the war would end quickly. In many of our conversations we discussed our vision of a Jewish homeland, a vision that became a dominant force and theme in my life. The open air and the millions of stars provided the perfect environment for me to think and formulate my political views. It had not required prolonged exposure to the real world for me to understand that a communist society did not include a safe place for Jews. Communist leadership seemed to be, to all intents and purposes, a dictatorship cloaked in grandiose promises of reform. I understood from my recent experiences that the economic hardship in Russia was the result not only of war, but also of a controlled economy that did not provide incentives to inspire hard work. My commitment to Zionism also became crystallized during those months in the Polish military. General Anders was supported by the British government and the Allied forces. Publicly, Anders claimed that Jews were accepted and treated fairly in his army but, privately, he encouraged antisemitic behavior. This only reinforced my belief that Jews needed an independent homeland.

The most blatant antisemitic experience I had was one afternoon, as I was sitting outside my tent in a rare relaxing moment. An officer suddenly walked up to me and started calling me derogatory names, including "dirty Jew." I was so incensed that I disregarded protocol, which prohibited a soldier to talk back to someone of superior rank, and I called him a "dirty Pole." This angry exchange culminated with the officer physically attacking me and threatening me with a dishonorable discharge. While I was not worried about the stigma of being discharged, I was extremely concerned about the effect such a discharge would have on my plans to leave Russia. When I realized that this man could ruin everything for me, I calmed down and silently vowed to do everything in my power to persevere until I could make my escape and reach Palestine.

Toward the end of basic training, our unit was scheduled to relocate out of Russia and join the British forces stationed in Iran. Some of the soldiers in the unit were excited about the prospect of finally entering the war, but Adam and I were excited about moving one step closer to Palestine. When our orders came to pack up our base camp and move out, we loaded our gear onto small cramped boats and sailed across the Caspian Sea to the port of Pachlevi in Iran.

After setting up camp, Adam and I wandered off to explore the area. Pachlevi was a beautiful port surrounded by soft, sandy beaches. It was our first time walking freely outside of the Soviet Union and it was exhilarating to be surrounded by a new environment. Adam and I walked along the beaches and met two Persian children selling eggs. Neither of us had seen or tasted eggs in many months, so we bought two dozen and decided to have a feast. We cooked the eggs over an open fire and gorged ourselves on the most delicious omelets I have ever tasted! Today, Adam and I still laugh about how many eggs we consumed that afternoon on the beaches of Pachlevi.

Not long after we landed on the shores of Pachlevi, we learned that our unit had been ordered to change direction. Instead of heading through Iraq toward Palestine, we were ordered to move to Khanaqin on the Iran-Iraq border. From there we were scheduled to meet the Polish soldiers returning from Egypt and Palestine, reorganize our units, and mobilize to the front lines in Italy. When Adam and I heard about this change, we were devastated. Our plan to use the army as a vehicle to reach Palestine was now in jeopardy. Our only hope was to desert from the army while we were still stationed in our camp in Iran.

Chapter Twelve

When our unit arrived in Khanaqin, the Polish forces had already taken over the town by erecting a military camp the size of a large village. Thousands of soldiers were getting ready to move to Italy. There seemed to be no hope that our unit would cross over the desert, in the direction of Palestine, before moving toward the frontlines.

Our first free afternoon was also the first day of *Rosh Hashanah* (the Jewish New Year). Adam and I left the army base and walked around until we found a small synagogue where we cautiously took seats in back of the sanctuary. We listened to the familiar Hebrew prayers recited to unfamiliar melodies when a man approached us and tried to say something in Arabic. After a few incomprehensible sentences, he pointed to the correct page in the prayer book and sat down. When the service was over, this same man returned and tried to communicate with us again. With bits of Hebrew and some English, we managed to exchange a few words and finally understood that he wanted to invite us to his home for dinner!

I will never forget the sight of that dinner table. It was beautifully laid with a white cloth and decorated with many colorful tropical fruits and vegetables that I had never seen before. It looked so appealing that I wanted to try each and every one. When I stopped gaping at the table, I became aware that the men were sitting in the living room while all the women were preparing the food in the kitchen. We could hear them giggle through the hanging beads that separated the rooms and, occasionally, one of them would peek her head through the curtain to catch a glimpse of Adam and me in our uniforms.

We sat on pillows on the floor and talked with the men for many hours. Communication became easier as we grew accustomed to mixing our different languages with the only emphasis on being understood. We talked about the war, about the hope of creating a Jewish state and about the curious reality of our being so different, and yet so similar, as Jews. We stayed far longer than our leave from the army permitted and I became worried that we would get into trouble and perhaps jeopardize our few freedoms from the unit. Thankfully, no one caught us and we returned to our tents unobserved.

Over dinner that night, a bond was created between Adam and myself, and this wonderful Sephardic family. They welcomed us into their home as though we were family members. Regardless of the fact that our customs and Jewish observances were so dissimilar, we developed a trust that felt familiar and warm. On that night there was no mention of our plan to desert the army, but I believe the thought crossed all of our minds.

We met the same family on the following day and, on this occasion, we mentioned our desire to start new lives in

Eretz Israel (Palestine). Over another delicious dinner, we explained that Adam had just received orders to travel to Baghdad as an army translator and this seemed like a perfect opportunity for us to get to Iraq and leave the base unnoticed. We needed help buying me a train ticket, and we needed to formulate a plan so that Adam and I could meet up in the city and make contact with the Jewish underground. Our friends invited us to meet a Jewish man who was planning a business trip to Baghdad, and he agreed to help us by purchasing my train ticket. He also agreed to act as a silent guardian for the length of the train ride and, if possible, prevent any unexpected trouble. Once we had both arrived in the city, we planned to meet in the courtyard of this man's hotel and make our next move.

On the agreed-upon evening, I left my army tent knowing I would never return. I arrived at the Jewish family's home and they helped disguise me as a poor Arab villager by dressing me in an old shirt, baggy pants, and sandals. We agreed that I would pretend to be deaf and dumb so as to avoid any problems arising from my ignorance of Muslim rituals and my inability to speak Arabic. The family gathered around me in a way that was reminiscent of the night I had left Makow, almost three years earlier. We were very emotional and, although we had only known each other a few days, we hugged and kissed like family. The man gave me three silver coins and warned me that if I got into any trouble, I should use this money as a bribe. He winked and said confidingly that in Iraq it was safe to assume that a bribe would work in almost any difficult situation.

Now, there was no turning back. By not returning to the military camp, I was burning the bridge that connected me to the known evils and relative safety of the Anders' army. After all these years, I was about to embark on the journey that might really lead me to Palestine — and I was terrified. Not only was I abandoning my position in the army, but I was entering the civilian world as a Jew disguised as an indigent Arab villager. At that time, the Jews of Iraq were living in terrible fear of antisemitic violence. If I had been discovered, I would surely have been killed. But while my life was in danger, so were the lives of the people who courageously swallowed their fear to help us. To this day, I am quite sentimental when I think of their courage and kindness.

Chapter Thirteen

My guide picked me up and took me to the train station but, after he bought my ticket, we did not speak for the remainder of the journey. He chose a seat in the same car as me, but far enough away so that no connection could be made between us. Not long after the train left the station, the inspectors passed through the compartments asking for tickets. This first inspection passed without a problem. When the conductor approached me, I pretended to be half asleep and simply handed him my ticket. He handed it back and left me alone.

Well into the night, another routine inspection began, but this time they were asking to see passports. As the inspection started in my compartment, I started to feel nervous and drained. I needed to figure out how to pass this next inspection, but I also desperately needed to lie down and rest. I decided to stretch out on the floor beside my seat. I felt very groggy when the inspector bent down to shake my arm and asked to see my passport. I pretended to still be asleep, but he would not leave me alone so I found my ticket and showed it to him. Since I had no passport, I acted as if I didn't understand what else he wanted and, finally, he went away. A few moments after he left, I saw him walk over to a police officer.

The policeman came to my seat and asked for my ticket and passport. When I pretended I didn't understand, he leaned on the chair in front of me with his knees at eye-level and his rifle, quite obviously, between his legs. I had to think fast so I reached into my pocket and felt for the silver coins. I pulled one coin out and started playing with it. As it became obvious the policeman saw my wordless offer, he changed positions and sat down beside me with his jacket open and his pockets easily accessible. I knew my bribe had been accepted, so I casually put the coin in his pocket. Afterward, I expected him to go away, but he didn't budge! He just kept sitting there, waiting for more, so I pulled out another coin. This time, I put it inside his coat and, just to make sure he felt it, I turned my hand to the right and then I turned my hand to the left. Then, very slowly, I let it fall with a clang against the other coin in his pocket. After a moment or two, he got up and left.

A few more hours passed, the sun was slowly lighting the sky and another ticket inspection started. The inspector started walking down the aisle, but I knew that I could not afford to take any more chances. As soon as he entered my compartment, I moved into the next one. When he entered the next compartment, I moved again. I kept my eye on him, and I kept moving one car ahead of him for the duration of his inspection. All the while I was accidentally stomping and tripping on parcels and sleeping passengers. People were growing quite impatient with me. Luckily, in the middle of moving through the compartments, the train came to a complete stop. I got off and re-boarded at the opposite end where I found a seat and waited.

More time passed and I saw that an inspection was starting again. I knew it was unlikely that there would be any more unexpected train stops, so once again I watched the inspector walk through the compartments. As he walked forward, I kept one car ahead of him. I kept moving from car to car but, finally, I found myself in the last compartment. I opened the door to keep moving forward, but I was stuck. In front of me was the locomotive and in back of me was the inspector. Without thinking, I stepped outside the train and closed the door. I then climbed onto the roof of the train and started crawling in the opposite direction, jumping from car to car while trying to keep my balance. I got to the other end of the train, climbed down, opened the door, and went inside. Breathless, I sat down and waited.

With dawn drawing near, I noticed that most of the men were kneeling to perform their morning prayers so, in order to avoid suspicion, I copied their motions. I knelt down, faced the same direction, and put my forehead on the ground as if I were bending to Mecca. I, evidently, succeeded in my charade because after the prayers, I was invited to share food with the group of Muslim men. I was frightened that they would discover I was not really an Arab, so I made a few guttural noises and moved forward to the next car.

Once again I found myself in the compartment with my silent guardian. We had not exchanged a single word for the length of the trip, but it was obvious that he had been watching me. As the train approached Baghdad we made eye contact and, at the appropriate moment, I followed him off the train. As soon as we were out of the station we were both relieved. He hailed a cab and gave me a lift to his hotel, where I planned to meet Adam.

Chapter Fourteen

When I think about the events of my life fifty years ago, I am often amazed at how oblivious I was to the dangers at that time. In retrospect, I realize how recklessly I behaved, driven by my desire to get to Palestine and away from the Nazis and the Polish antisemites. Desertion, in the middle of a war, would surely have lead to my execution. Today, when I consider this possibility, I am astounded at how secondary it seemed to me at the time. I was foolish and young, and I am amazed as I re-tell the story that the possibly fatal repercussions for my actions did not prevent me from going through with my plans.

We arrived at the hotel. My guardian checked in and let me sleep in his room. The hotel was a small, three-story building, and each room opened onto a long, continuous balcony oriented inward, facing a traditional Eastern-style courtyard. The room was on the third floor of the hotel. It was fairly empty and had only two thin cots. I later learned that the furnishings in these rooms were kept to a minimum so commercial traders could store their goods before returning to their towns and villages.

Once I was alone in the hotel room, I collapsed from sheer exhaustion and, after a few hours, I woke up in a cold sweat. I had fallen into such a deep sleep that I had forgotten where I was, and it took a minute to re-orient myself and remember everything that had happened in the previous twenty-four hours.

I walked over to the balcony and peered down onto the beautiful, sunny courtyard. I watched the hustle and bustle of the merchants and travelers sitting at the round tables. One man, in particular, caught my eye. He was sitting very casually, balancing his weight on the back legs of his chair, with one hand in his pocket. He wore a white jacket, white pants, and a tropical helmet. He looked like the perfect image of freedom and relaxation, reading a book and basking in the late morning sun. Then, as I looked a little closer, I realized that the man was Adam!

I left my room and hurried down to the courtyard to greet him. I was ecstatic that we had both successfully arrived at the hotel. I was so happy to see him that we hugged and greeted like brothers. I couldn't believe how good he looked. He was dressed impeccably and had erased all traces of his former military self. It was very emotional for me to see him out of uniform. After the ruckus of our initial meeting subsided, we found an inconspicuous corner and proceeded to talk about our experiences on arriving in Baghdad and how to make contact with the Jewish underground.

We sat together while Adam recounted his adventures

of the last few days. Before he left the base on official army business, many of the soldiers gave him watches they wanted him to fix or sell in the city so, on the first morning, he left the base claiming that he would attend to the soldiers' watch repairs. He hailed a cab and while, at that moment, he intended to abandon the Anders' army forever, when he got into the taxi he realized that he didn't have any idea where to go! It was too early to meet me at the hotel, so he needed to kill time. The taxi driver, who had given hundreds of rides to visiting military officers, assumed that Adam wanted to go to an officer's brothel but was too shy to ask, so within moments of trying to go AWOL, Adam found himself at an army brothel!

Adam stayed at the brothel and had a great time for two or three days. During that time, he would occasionally walk to the hotel to see if I had arrived. When I hadn't arrived by the third day, he grew nervous. After a couple of days, it was safe to assume that if I had managed to get away from the base, my arrival was imminent. Since he knew he had to change to civilian clothes to avoid being caught, he contacted a man who could be trusted to sell him clothes consisting of white pants, a white jacket, a hat, and shoes. Then, he bought a book and pretended to be a rich businessman while waiting for me in the hotel courtyard.

As we talked, we realized that I also needed a change of clothes to avoid arousing suspicion. More importantly, we needed to make the appropriate connections with the underground to gain entry to Palestine. I felt so relieved to see Adam that it was only much later that I realized how much further we still needed to go before we could think of ourselves as truly free. Until that moment, it seemed like arriving in Baghdad was the most important thing in the world. In reality, it was only one small step toward our goal.

Our first thought was to contact the rabbi in the local community. Adam had learned where the synagogue was located, so we walked to the area while maintaining a distance from each other to avoid arousing suspicion. We were worried about drawing attention to ourselves since I was still dressed as an indigent Arab villager, and Adam had the appearance of a stately English gentleman — although he later confessed that his shoes were one and a half sizes too small. When we finally found the rabbi, we told him our story but he responded with terror and concern that our presence would jeopardize the safety of his community. He refused to help us and asked us to leave the synagogue immediately. Basically, he threw us out into the street.

We only had one other possible contact. My guardian had given me the name of a "Dr. Rosenfeld," who, supposedly, had connections to the Jewish underground. I had his name but no address so, devastated by the rabbi's response, we walked around the city in search of a medical office with Dr. Rosenfeld's name. We walked up and down the streets for many hours, unsure what we would do if this last hope were dashed when, finally, we stopped in front of an optometrist's office with the name "Dr. Rosenfeld" on the door. I waited outside while Adam went in to meet the doctor.

Adam saw Dr. Rosenfeld right away, and in an excited mixture of Yiddish and English, he tried to tell our story and ask for help, but Dr. Rosenfeld quieted him down immediately. His secretary was an Arab woman and, at that time, no one knew who could be trusted. The doctor took Adam into a back room where he quietly agreed that he would try to help us but that we would have to return for some further questioning after dark when the office was closed. When Adam came outside with the good news, I was thrilled. We both thought that it was understandable that Dr. Rosenfeld wanted to question us, so with renewed hope, we eagerly waited for night to fall.

At our meeting later that evening, Dr. Rosenfeld noticeably warmed to Adam and me after I started speaking to him in Hebrew. We told him abbreviated versions of our escape stories from Poland. He then explained that the Jewish community in Baghdad was divided between the old school and the new, activist school. The old school was dominated by the honorable rabbi who cooperated with the authorities in order to protect his congregation and, therefore, would not provide shelter for fleeing Jewish refugees. The new, activist school was dominated by a young group of Jewish activists who had strong Zionist feelings. It was the latter group who might be willing to help.

Dr. Rosenfeld had contacted a member of this younger, Zionist group after our visit earlier that day and, after a few moments, a tall, lean boy and his sister arrived at the doctor's office. They were obviously well educated and asked us a series of questions before they were satisfied that our story was true. After they believed that we were Jewish boys who had managed to escape from Poland and wanted to live in Palestine, they made arrangements for us to sleep in the attic of the old synagogue. We agreed to wait there until they could make contact with the Haganah (the Jewish underground resistance movement) in Palestine. In the meantime, they would bring us food and a change of clothes.

The next day happened to be *Erev Yom Kippur* (the Eve of the Day of Atonement), so while Adam and I hid in the attic, we watched the community's *Kol Nidre* service. After the next day of services and fasting, we were invited to break the fast with a family from the Zionist group. That meal was the only time we left the synagogue attic, and the many days in hiding passed very, very slowly. I was very uncomfortable and nervous during the entire time because we simply could not be sure that the Zionist group could help us — and if they could not get us one step closer to Palestine, I had no idea what we would do next.

Days after the holidays ended, we were told that Dr. Rosenfeld had arranged a meeting with Enzo Sereni[1] and Moshe Dayan,[2] two men from Palestine who could possibly help us. They were staying in a modern, white hotel with a beautiful garden in the middle of a circular driveway leading to the main entrance. We stood outside the hotel for a few moments before Adam went inside to call the operator and ask for Enzo Sereni's room. Mr. Sereni came down to the lobby and started talking to Adam in a broken Yiddish. After a few moments, they

110

switched to English. Adam remembers that after he told the short version of our decision to desert the army, Sereni used the well-known Yiddish expression: *"meshuganer!"*

Even though our story was so unusual, Sereni wanted proof that it was really true and felt uncomfortable talking inside the hotel. They came outside and I joined in the discussion. When I started speaking Hebrew, it instantly gave us credibility. But Sereni also wanted proof that we were really from Poland, so Adam mentioned the names of one or two Zionist activists from his small town. One name he mentioned was of a local political figure affiliated with a party Sereni opposed, but it also confirmed that we were legitimate. A "spy" would not have known the name of such a relatively unknown person. Sereni finally accepted our story and promised to contact us when his colleague, Dayan, arrived in Baghdad.

Within a day or two we were told to go back to the hotel at a designated hour. We walked over to the grand white building, went inside the lobby and up to Sereni's room and waited. Suddenly, Dayan burst through the door, muddy and exhausted. He had obviously just finished some type of "operation" because he tore the dirty shirt off his back and only gruffly greeted us on his way into the bathroom. After he washed up, he spoke to us briefly and told us to return the following night prepared to join a bus convoy that was returning to Palestine. He gave specific instructions on when and where to meet, and we left the hotel.

The following night, we met Dayan at the designated location and got into a car with him and a driver. The four of us drove to the edge of an army base where Indian soldiers had been stationed to fight alongside the Allies. Our mission was to fill suitcases with military arms stored at the army base and then get away from the base as quickly as possible. Dayan guided us through a fence, across a road lined with barbed wire, and through muddy ditches until we reached the base. We filled the suitcases and then made our way to a big parking lot where five or six buses were stationed. Dayan made very cursory introductions to one or two drivers and quickly left the area.

The bus company, Egged, was transporting soldiers from Palestine to military installations in Iraq. Buses arrived in Baghdad filled with British soldiers and were then sent back to Palestine empty. Adam and I noticed that the buses had a number of coffins on board. The Haganah had manufactured documents indicating that these coffins contained the deceased bodies of soldiers, which were highly contaminated. In reality, these coffins were loaded with weapons and were being sent back to help the resistance effort in Palestine. When Dayan left the area, we tried to board one of these buses, but we were stopped by the driver. He absolutely refused to be responsible for hiding Polish deserters at the risk of jeopardizing the entire underground operation and insisted that we leave the base immediately.

Adam and I reached an all-time low. We were so close, yet so far from actually reaching Palestine. It was almost sunrise when we turned around and walked the many miles back to the center of Baghdad. We attached ourselves to a group of peasants so we wouldn't attract attention and, once again, went in search of Dr. Rosenfeld.

We found Dr. Rosenfeld that morning, and he arranged for us to join another bus convoy. This time, however, we planned to disguise ourselves as British soldiers so as to make our presence less obvious. On our second attempt, we met Dayan at the same place and traveled down the same road to the same military installation at the Indian camp. Once again, we arrived at the parking lot with the convoy of buses but, this time, we successfully boarded one of them and waited. After a short while, the drivers saw us and tried to make us leave but I absolutely refused. I was adamant and started aggressively arguing in Hebrew that there was absolutely no way we were turning back. Finally, a driver named Shapiro, the son of the famous *Shomer* ("Watchman") Avraham Shapiro from Petach Tikvah, volunteered to take full responsibility for us. The other drivers who were uneasy about our presence could claim they knew nothing about us and, after considerable debate, it was decided that we would ride with Shapiro in his bus.[3]

In Israel, on Independence Day in 1993, I attended a memorial service for fallen soldiers with my friend and colleague, (Ret.) General Menachem Einan. At the end of the service, Menachem introduced the man standing next to him as Eldad Shapiro. His face was very familiar to me but, for a moment or two, I couldn't remember where I had seen him before. Finally, rather shyly, I asked him if he and his family were from Petach Tikvah. When he replied that he was, I asked him whether his father had been an Egged bus driver in 1942. He looked at me curiously and said that his father had, in fact, been an Egged bus driver in 1942. Then I said...so you are the grandson of Avraham Shapiro? When he told me that he was, I told him that he was a carbon copy of his father at the same age! He looked astounded, so I explained to him that his father was the driver who had risked his life to drive Adam and me to Palestine in September 1942.

The bus ride to Palestine from the outskirts of Baghdad took about five days and four nights. We drove in a long convoy of ten buses in a straight line along the flat desert terrain. The buses stayed on a single dirt road parallel to an oil pipeline, which ran the entire length of the desert. Adam and I sat together disguised in British army coveralls. Adam recalls that he spent most of the time barefoot — rubbing his aching feet! We had no identity documents. Between us, the most valuable thing we carried was Adam's English dictionary. If the caravan were searched, we would be in terrible trouble. At night, when the buses stopped, the soldiers from the other buses, also returning with the convoy, made contact with each other. Adam mingled freely because he could speak English and pretend to be a soldier — but I could not. Adam even entertained the soldiers by singing songs, while

114

I spent the time pretending to be a mechanic working under the hood of the bus.

As we approached the border of Palestine, there was a debate on whether we should cross the border of the Jordan River inside the bus or on foot. Shapiro had already stalled our bus in order to gain time before we reached the checkpoint. We all agreed that it would be safer for the operation if Adam and I crossed on foot, so we disembarked a fair distance from the bridge and scrambled to the edge of the river. We hid in overgrown bushes and watched the bus convoy cross the B'not Ya'acov bridge into Palestine. Finally, we waded across the river and climbed up on the other side of the river bank into Eretz Israel.

I wish I could say that at that moment when we crossed the river into Eretz Israel, we were overwhelmed by a sense of enormous excitement — but we were not. We could not permit ourselves to feel any great excitement because we were still in danger. Dayan had promised to notify Kibbutz Maoz Chaim of our impending arrival and someone was supposed to come to pick us up, but no one seemed to be there waiting to greet us. We lay hiding for quite a while and then, finally, we heard the rickety clickety-clack of an old kibbutz truck driving south of the bridge where we had crossed.[4] The driver, whom I remember was wearing an old cotton hat and sandals, stopped the truck and got out to look around. After a few moments, we knew that he was probably the man sent to pick us up, so we emerged from the bushes and moved toward the truck.

115

1   Enzo Sereni later parachuted on a heroic mission across enemy
    lines and was captured in German territory by the Nazis. He was
    killed in Dachau in 1944.
2   Moshe Dayan became a great military and political hero and
    played an active role in the establishment of the State of Israel and
    its later administration.
3   Moshe Dayan remembers this incident in Baghdad in his
    autobiography as follows:

> In the evening we went into the Jewish Quarter and met the
> people who were active in the community and anxious to
> leave for Palestine. They asked me to smuggle into
> Palestine two young Jewish refugees from Poland who had
> managed to escape from the Nazis and to make their way to
> Iran. From there they had arrived in Baghdad, another step
> en route to Palestine. I agreed, and we organized an
> "exchange operation." I returned to the camp that night
> and crept out again the following evening with the suitcases
> of weapons. I gave them to the Haganah cell and took in
> exchange the two refugees, whom we dressed in British
> army uniforms.
>
> I had to make the return journey to Palestine in another
> bus. The drivers were reluctant to take the risk of
> transporting "illegal immigrants" in their vehicles. But one
> driver finally agreed. A *sabra* from Petach Tikva, a suburb
> near Tel Aviv, he was the son of Avraham Shapiro, the
> famed "Watchman" of the early pioneer days, when a
> colorful band of mounted Jewish guards would roam the
> area of isolated Jewish farm settlements challenging Arab
> marauders and helping to maintain security.

Moshe Dayan, *Moshe Dayan; Story of My Life* (New York:
William Morrow and Company, Inc., 1976), p. 77.

4   Moshe Dayan continues in his recollection that the trip went
    without incident and says, "I left the refugees at Kibbutz Maoz
    Chaim." *Ibid.*

PART TWO

1943–1950

Chapter Fifteen

Upon arriving at the kibbutz, after years of running and living in a constant state of fear and anxiety, I finally felt that I could unburden my heart and mind. I had dreamed of the day I would arrive, alive, in Eretz Israel. The constant stress of the last few years was made easier by my constant desire to achieve that goal, so, when I first arrived in the kibbutz dining hall, it was as if all my dreams had come true.

My vision of living in Israel had always included the romantic notion of living an agricultural life, working the soil, and even riding donkeys through the fields! It was a dream of a life completely and utterly different from the one I had known in Poland. Once I set foot on the kibbutz, surrounded by welcoming Jewish faces, I felt comforted by the warm pioneer spirit and the flood of Hebrew words spoken by people committed to the creation of a Jewish state. Standing in the safety of that dining room, I felt the emotional drain of each and every perilous moment since I had left Poland in 1939, and the high of having successfully attained my goal. I had arrived. I could claim a personal victory over the Nazi forces.

After an overwhelming greeting by the kibbutz members, a young man showed Adam and me to our tent, a luxurious accommodation that contained two narrow cots with clean sheets. He then took us to the laundry room and gave us freshly washed work clothes and sun hats. He also showed us the outdoor shower where we washed and, finally, returned to our new lodgings for some much needed rest.

The following morning, we woke up early and joined the kibbutz members for a day of work in the fields. After months of guarding our every move, the freedom we experienced working among Jews was an indescribable luxury. I have some wonderful memories of those first few weeks, particularly of long mornings enveloped by the intense heat of the Jordan Valley and the feeling of accomplishment after completing physically challenging agricultural work. I also have vivid memories of returning home to shower in the outdoor stall near our tent. I loved the way the sun shined brightly as the cool water splashed over my body.

In those early weeks, one incident in particular has stayed etched in my mind as a moment of true awakening to my new life. I was outside showering, when I heard a beautiful female voice singing a Hebrew song. That glorious moment of spontaneous song was the symbol of my new freedom. I was so elated by the music that I realized how long it had been since I had felt safe enough to savor a romantic thought upon hearing a woman sing.

Chapter Sixteen

During our first few weeks on the kibbutz, Adam and I made efforts to contact our family members. I had managed to hold on to Uncle Nathan's business card throughout my years of running and, although it was crumpled and frayed at the edges from nervous handling, it was a cherished possession, which I guarded from total decay. This business card was the embodiment of Uncle Nathan's great financial success in England, and it suggested the possibility of contacting the rest of my family through his home in London.

Uncle Nathan had left his father's cabinet-making business in Poland in the late 1800s, and set off to seek his fortune in the United States. On the voyage to America, the ship stopped in England where he attended religious services for the Jewish holidays. After services, he was invited home for a traditional meal with a family from the community, who also owned a successful cabinet-making business. This family also had a beautiful daughter. Uncle Nathan soon married her and built up a successful furniture business in exotic woods, veneers, and custom-made pieces. Every few years, he would return to Poland to visit his mother and sisters in a flurry of riches and splendor and would be driven into town in a big fancy car, loaded with gifts. As I have mentioned earlier, when Nathan's daughter Esther got married, in 1933, he bought train and boat tickets for my grandmother, aunt, and mother. In those days traveling to England for the occasion of a wedding was such an extraordinary event that everybody talked about it with a mixture of awe and envy for months afterward.

In the early 1960s, my wife, Stephanie, and I returned to England to visit my cousin Esther and her husband, Sid. We visited their home in London and saw footage from movies taken by Esther's brother, Alfred, from their wedding, in 1933. It was an emotional experience to see my mother and aunt "live" on film. Over the years, I have tried to accumulate photographs of my family and this movie was absolutely priceless to me. Cousin Alfred graciously agreed to make me a copy, which I still cherish to this day.

On that same visit, I learned that Esther and Sid were planning to remodel and modernize the furnishings in their home for the first time in thirty years. They wanted to empty the house of everything, including their piano, and start afresh. All of the furniture had been custom made by Esther's father, Nathan, on the occasion of her wedding. At that time Stephanie and I already had two children, so I asked if I could have the piano as a memento of Uncle

Nathan and for my children to play. Within weeks after we returned to Canada, Esther and Sid shipped us the beautiful baby grand, custom built by Nathan for their wedding thirty years earlier. We still have this piano in our living room today.

Another possible way to contact my family was through my Uncle Sam in South Africa. Sam, my mother's youngest brother, had left Poland in the early 1920's, with another brother, my Uncle Usher. Their first destination was France where, I am told, they lived in poverty and slept under bridges. Over time, however, both brothers became prominent in the fashion industry. Sam was very ambitious, so he left France for the undiscovered world of opportunity in South Africa. I made contact with Sam, since he lived in the free world, but I did not attempt to write to Usher in German-occupied Paris. I also did not risk writing to my other uncle, Mordechai, who lived in war-ravaged Belgium. After the war, I learned that Usher had been killed in Auschwitz, but his wife and children had survived. Mordechai and his entire family were also killed in Nazi concentration camps.

In Johannesburg, Uncle Sam had developed a successful fashion business with many showrooms. He used to correspond with my mother and send her pictures of his enormous house and his many servants. Although I had never seen him, I had developed a great respect for Sam and looked forward to the day when I would meet him.

As I waited for my uncle's response, Adam also made attempts to contact his family. He wrote to his Aunt Gonja, who was a doctor living in Palestine. When Gonja heard of Adam's arrival, in the middle of war, it seemed so impossible that she sent a scout to verify the news. One day, after working in the fields, Adam received a visit from a man named Zoma whom he knew from childhood. After their joyful greeting, this man confirmed to Gonja that her nephew Adam was indeed on Kibbutz Maoz Chaim. Zoma also reported that Adam had arrived in Palestine with a friend who *looked* just like Adam's twin brother who had been killed a few years earlier. Not long after that visit, Aunt Gonja arrived at the kibbutz with an enormous package filled with two of everything — one for Adam and one for me. Two sweaters, two pairs of pants, two shirts, and two pairs of shoes! I was deeply touched by her generosity and I will always remember her warm and immediate acceptance of me as a member of the family.

Aunt Gonja was an incredible woman. Physically, she was quite plain with a long face and somewhat masculine features, but her generous spirit always made her dark and wrinkled face seem warm and attractive. She was born in Russia, where her father had been a well-respected rabbi, but she left before World War I to study medicine in Switzerland. On a visit home to Russia during the war, Gonja was kidnapped by a group of nationalist right-wing antisemites who were attempting to establish an independent Ukraine. This group of militants needed a doctor on staff and forcibly demanded her services as a physician. During her captivity, however, Gonja and an officer of the nationalist group fell in love. When the war ended, he followed her to Palestine, where they lived together in Kfar Saba. Gonja lived with this man until the day he died but, because he was not Jewish, they never married or had children.

Gonja had a gallery of people whom she helped throughout the country. When she first arrived in Palestine, she was not permitted to practice medicine independently because her license was from Switzerland. After a short time, however, she met Dr. Hirsch Rozal, the primary physician for the Arab communities. Dr. Rozal needed Gonja's help because Arab men would not permit a male doctor to examine their wives and daughters. Gonja quickly became a trusted midwife and physician throughout the Arab community and people would travel for days in order to receive her care.

It was Gonja's sage advice that helped direct Adam and me to continue our university studies after we had adjusted to life on kibbutz. With her help, we discovered that the Hebrew University in Jerusalem would be the best choice for Adam to pursue his interest in literature, while the Technion in Haifa was the best place for me to study engineering and architecture.

After an initial adjustment, Adam and I grew accustomed to our free but routine lives on the kibbutz. We were impatient to see the rest of the country, but we were not permitted to leave the kibbutz until we received our identity papers from the Jewish Agency. While we waited for our papers, I recall feeling that the kibbutz was becoming a little confining. Living on Maoz Chaim was comfortable and pleasant, but it did not take long for us to realize that it would not be more than a stopover on our continuing journey toward greater freedom and independence.

In February 1943, Adam and I received our identity cards. The same day we hitchhiked to the nearest town, Afula, where we noticed a kiosk selling fresh juice and chocolate. Neither of us had tasted any chocolate in years, so we bought five or six bars and spent the afternoon savoring them and walking around town — in no rush and with no cause to look over our shoulders.

Adam and I also took a day trip to the beaches of Tel Aviv. I remember standing on a pier overlooking the sea on a brisk winter day. We stood there for a long time and reminisced about the last time we had stood by a sea, the Caspian Sea, when we were soldiers in the Anders' army. At that time the open water had felt like the closest thing to true freedom either of us had experienced in months. It was a symbol that we were on our way to Palestine and beyond the reaches of the oppressive atmosphere in Russia. That day in Tel Aviv, overlooking the Mediterranean, we recalled those feelings and compared them to the immense joy we now felt, as civilians, ready and excited to start our education in Palestine.

Chapter Seventeen

In March 1943, Adam and I separated to pursue our respective preparatory courses for university. Aunt Gonja had many contacts in the Russian-speaking community in Haifa, and, through her connections, I found accommodation on the ground floor of a stone house. The woman who owned the apartment spoke very little Hebrew, but she was very kind and permitted me to sleep on a cot in her kitchen. She also introduced me to a man who owned a Ford Motor Company garage, where I got my first job as an assistant car mechanic.

During my first few months in Haifa, I was very busy working and preparing for university. In my job as an assistant mechanic, I learned skills required for basic car repairs, and I made enough money to cover my living expenses. When I wasn't working, I studied Hebrew and other subjects required for admission to the Technion program in engineering and architecture. My tutor, Mr. Goldberg, was a short man with a warm jovial manner. I enjoyed learning with him and have fond memories of how he delighted in my progress. It is certainly in large part due to his help that I was able to gain entrance to the Technion in September 1943.

During those spring and summer months of 1943, when I was not busy with work or my preparatory studies, I spent some time with the Becker family. The Beckers were from Riga — no relation to the Becker family from Luninietz. They were very well educated and would frequently invite me for dinner and lively conversation about politics. I also became friendly with the Biberstein twins, who were about my age and originally from Poland. Most of my social time, however, except for the occasional visit to meet Adam at Aunt Gonja's house in Kfar Saba, was reserved for special visits to the Rosenberg family in Bitan Aaron, near Kfar Vitkin.

Before the war, the Rosenbergs had lived in the same building as my family in Makow. I had always thought of the Rosenbergs as true Zionists, who had given up everything in order to move to Eretz Israel. I remember that in the late 1930s, before the war, Mr. Rosenberg resigned from his very good job at a flour mill and sold most of his family's possessions for £1000 sterling. The official entry restrictions to Palestine did not apply if an independent immigrant could prove he had this sum. The Rosenbergs bought land on a *moshav* (agricultural settlement) in Bitan Aaron and started new lives as farmers. The day the Rosenbergs left Poland to make their courageous move, I remember how inspired my mother felt by their commitment to live in Eretz Israel.

Upon moving to Haifa, I learned that the Rosenbergs lived close by, and I started visiting them on weekends. They lived in an orchard with a wonderful garden and a big yard, where livestock ran freely. I loved visiting there and I

David and David Flatau

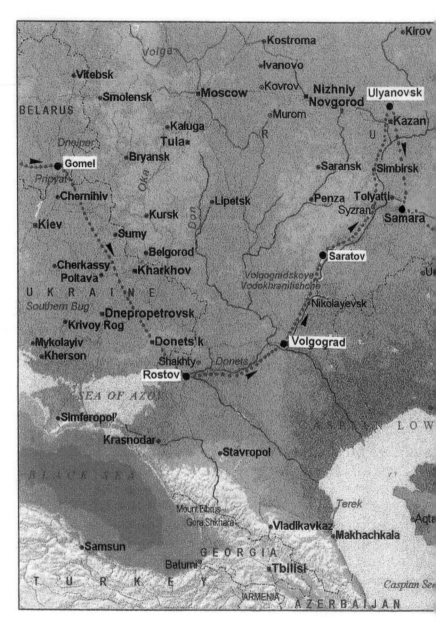

Escape from Gomel to Tashkent

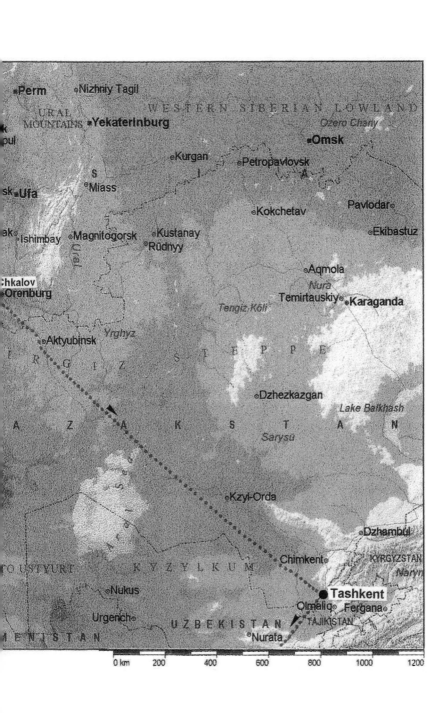

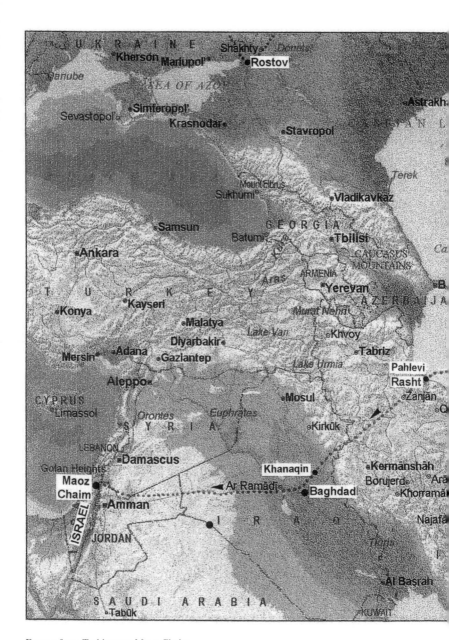

Escape from Tashkent to Maoz Chaim

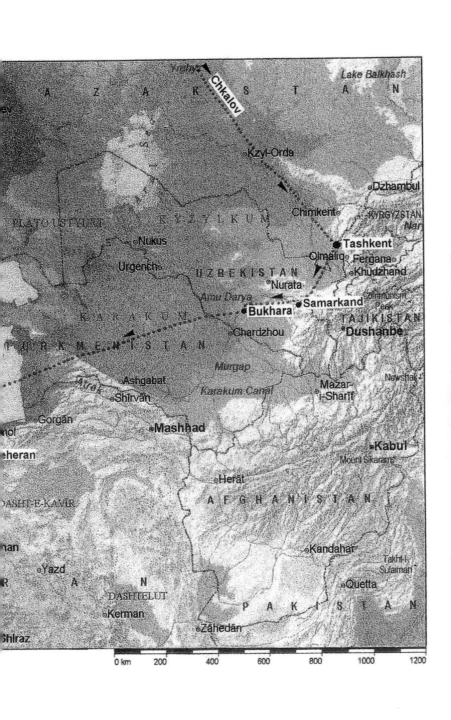

David upon his arrival in Israel

David — helping the Rosenbergs on Moshav Bitan Aharon

Dr. Gonya Fogel and Adam Gillon

David as a student at the Technion

David as a student at the Technion

David standing (second from left) with soccer team at the Technion

David with students on a field trip

David (front row, fourth from right) with class at the Riali School in Haifa, 1946.

David's brother, Ephraim,
his wife Miriam and
children, Moti and Aryeh

Uncle Nathan's
business card

A visit in London, England, with Uncle Nathan, his wife and daughter

David in Makow Maz, 1990

David and his two youngest daughters Naomi (left) and Danna, the author (right) at the monument commemorating the uprising in the Warsaw Ghetto, 1990

David at the Jewish cemetery in Bialystok, 1990

David, Danna (left) and Naomi (right), at a war memorial in Brest, 1990

always felt extremely welcome — it was like coming home. Being around them was familiar and easy. I used to help Mr. Rosenberg with his work in the orchard and, in those moments, working the land in my shorts, hat, and sandals, I felt that I was living the Zionist dream. When the work was complete, Mrs. Rosenberg would cook delicious meals, and the whole family would sit together to eat and sing Hebrew songs, while we kept alive the hope that the latest news from Europe did not apply to the people we loved.

On other occasions I would make the longer journey to Kfar Saba to visit Aunt Gonja. These trips were also extremely relaxing, because her small, single-story house was built low to the ground and surrounded and insulated by the thick trees of the orchard, which kept it cool in the summer and warm in the winter. The yard was always messy and full of livestock and, inside, the bare and simple furnishings were warm and welcoming. This atmosphere did wonders in replenishing my energy for the coming week.

When I received the news that I had been accepted to the Technion, I was thrilled. It was a real breakthrough in my new life. Unlike many refugees at the time who did not consider the idea of continuing their education important and who devoted themselves to earning money, I knew that I wanted to continue my education, and I was pleased that my hard work in the preparatory courses had paid off.

In August, before the school term began, I moved into a room in an apartment on Hehalutz Street, Number 9. The room had two single beds, and I shared it with Moshe, a fellow student in the architecture program at the Technion. When school started, I also had to continue working at odd jobs to make enough money for my expenses. At the same time, with the help of Moshe's expertise in English, I renewed my efforts to contact my Uncle Nathan in England and my Uncle Sam in South Africa. When Uncle Nathan finally wrote back, it was a surprisingly curt note requesting assurances that I was truly his nephew. Apparently, many refugees were contacting wealthy Jews outside the war zones and claiming to have family ties in order to receive financial support. I responded with a letter filled with details about my family in order to prove that my mother was really Nathan's sister and that I was really his nephew. Soon thereafter, Uncle Nathan sent me the generous gift of fifty English pounds, which I used to pay my accumulating debt of tuition and rent.

When Uncle Sam received my letter, he took an immediate interest in me and was excited to learn that I was studying at the Technion. We corresponded regularly and he started sending me a monthly stipend of five pounds sterling. This money was crucial to my daily existence and provided enormous help in my constant struggle to make ends meet. Uncle Sam also sent me regular packages of clothing he no longer wanted. Physically, we were similar in size, so his tailored shirts, pants and jackets fit me almost perfectly. I always kept myself neat and well groomed, but, in retrospect, I must have been quite a sight in my luxurious second-hand clothes! Occasionally, I would even sell a few items from these packages to help keep myself out of debt.

At that time finding money to pay for a decent meal was a constant struggle. On many early mornings, Moshe and I would go to a small dairy restaurant near our apartment, where the owner, Menashke, would cook omelets for us on credit. This little restaurant was a constant source of goodwill and comfort for me. Another place where we used to eat was the Histadrut (Union) dining room. This dining hall was operated for the workers of Haifa and was intended to provide nourishing meals at low and affordable prices. I could sustain myself by ordering a big bowl of soup and an unlimited amount of bread for one and a half piasters.

During those first years in school, I held down at least four or five part-time jobs. My main goal was always to make enough money to get the infamous stamp in my student identification book that indicated that my tuition was paid. Every student carried a brown book with his or her picture, identification, and a square stamp marking their payments for each semester. Without this stamp, no student was permitted to take exams or receive credit for class work, and it was always a scramble to make payments on time.

One of my jobs was as a counselor supervising children in a playground in a small city park in the afternoon. I also worked near the Haifa Bay as a *"gafir,"* an auxiliary policeman on a night shift. This job did not last more than a few months, because the night schedule was too exhausting after attending class all day, but the income was good, and I tried to keep it up for as long as I could.

After a while, I found another job as a "toast-master." This job started very early in the morning and was for a British officers' school located in a hotel on Mount Carmel. The hotel was owned by the Telch family, and my job was to arrive every morning and make toast for British officers. I must admit that I enjoyed watching high-ranking British intelligence officers line up behind my four toasters and wait patiently for me to brown their slices! I was also lucky, because Mrs. Telch often made me breakfast after my shift was over and would also pack me lunch for the day. The job also included bus fare for the ride up and down Mount Carmel. The only problem was that, by the time the officers finished breakfast and Mrs. Telch had prepared my food, I would inevitably arrive late or miss my first class of the day.

During the summer between my first and second years at the university, I found a job at the Tira military camp, where I was required to overhaul gearboxes and instruments for tanks and airplanes. Every morning, when it was still dark outside, a truck would pick up a group of workers at a designated spot and drive us to the factory. I used to stand on the back of the truck and watch deliveries being made at the small neighborhood stores. Often the deliveries arrived before the shops were open and I was amazed to see that no one would steal any of the produce waiting outside. In those days, doors were rarely closed and almost never locked. That trust between storekeepers and suppliers is a wonderful example of the pioneer spirit that infused the country at that time.

At the beginning of my second year at the Technion, I left my summer position at Tira and took another job at a factory associated with the university. The hours were compatible with my class schedule because I worked from early evening until very late at night. My obligations for this job involved working with hard metal, creating perfectly flat plates to be used as work surfaces for testing sensitive military equipment. While I busily worked and attended class, my social life also flourished. I became close friends with a group of students, all of whom had managed to escape from Poland and were united by a common background. Many of us joined the Haganah, hoping to develop a strong resistance against the British who were preventing the influx of Jews from Europe. I had only limited involvement in these underground activities but, when I wasn't working or studying, I would attend meetings at a training camp near Mishmar Ha'emek.

Chapter Eighteen

My group of friends from the Technion developed into a tight-knit family. We were all poor, and few of us had any relatives in Palestine. Each of us had been transplanted from our hometowns in Poland, had arrived as penniless refugees in Palestine, and had somehow managed to gain acceptance at university. Our excitement about the future and our *joie de vivre* seemed almost incongruous with the horrors of our pasts, with the war still ravaging Europe, and with the oppressive British rule in Palestine. We embraced a bohemian counter-culture lifestyle and, somehow, always managed to steal precious moments from our daily financial struggles to create a celebratory atmosphere while sitting on a beach, or over a single cup of coffee in a favorite café.

Sometimes on weekends and special occasions, a whole group of us would take the bus to the Kayat Beach, south of Haifa. We would spend the day lying on the sand and playing in the sun. As the sun set, we would take showers in the public changing rooms and gather outside on the restaurant terrace for an afternoon of song and dance based on the British custom of afternoon tea. Those were truly wonderful days when we enjoyed the luxury of our freedom and shared our hopes and dreams of undiscovered worlds, just beyond the sunset, waiting for us to explore and conquer.

On school days our meeting place was Café Atara, on the corner of Herzl and Balfour streets near the university. We would spend hours talking, sitting huddled together at small cramped tables. The newspapers were free so we could follow the daily news, and there was always someone debating the political issues of the day. I would often find my friend Tollek, impeccably dressed, sitting at a table, twirling his mustache and smoking his pipe. Tollek was a slightly controversial character because he liked to tell stories about his unbelievable adventures as a pilot before the war. I never really cared if the stories were true. I simply enjoyed them and Tollek's entertaining company. My friend Mietek was another colorful and slightly outrageous character whom I liked and respected. He displayed a kind of rebellious creativity — which had him drawing circles in a drafting class when the rest of us were drawing straight lines. He was a tall, lumbering man with a neatly groomed red beard and completely bald head. He had arrived in Israel before the war and enrolled as a student at the Technion. When the war broke out he joined the British Navy and, in a short time, was promoted from sailor to officer. In 1943, he was discharged and returned to Palestine to complete his studies. Mietek and I met at the Technion and because he was older and had been in the navy, he always seemed more mature and experienced than the rest of us.

Our group also included Celina, a very bright student in chemical engineering who was married to Bezalel. In 1948, Bezalel was killed in a battle for downtown Haifa. I vividly recall this tragedy, as it was the first time a member of our group was killed in the struggle for the State of Israel, and we were all profoundly shocked. Zosia was another very bright and determined student; she dated Mietek. Urek lived two houses away from me on Hehalutz Street and we frequently gathered at his apartment for a friendly game of poker. Two other friends I remember were Stasiek and another young man also named Mietek. They were not enrolled in the Technion, but went to law school instead.

I had one or two other special friends in the group, like Izio Rosen, who had been one of the few Jews in my unit in the Anders' army. As soldiers we had not been very close, so when Adam and I went AWOL I did not know if I would see him again. Ironically, a few weeks after Adam and I deserted our unit, the Anders' army changed its plan to go directly to Italy and made a stop in Palestine. Izio seized the opportunity to go AWOL and start a new life on kibbutz. Later he enrolled as a civil-engineering student at the Technion, where we met again.

On the kibbutz Izio met another good friend, Irka. They initially became friends because they both spoke an educated Polish and longed to converse in their native tongue. At that time, Poles spoke many languages and dialects which served as a type of social code. It was easy to determine a person's background and education after only a few sentences, and friendships were frequently formed within moments of meeting. Irka was wondering whether she should pursue her studies in engineering and architecture and, with Izio's help, she was soon enrolled at the Technion and became a member of our group. Irka was a beautiful woman with a sweet, melodic voice. Whenever we could, we would encourage her to sing, and occasionally she would display her musical talent by performing for the entire school.

In 1945, I invited Adam to take a break from his work in Jerusalem and visit me in Haifa for the Purim ball. At this party Adam met Irka and fell madly in love. Adam had just completed his studies at the Hebrew University and had been awarded a scholarship to complete his dissertation. For months after the ball, Adam would make the long trek to Haifa to visit Irka on every possible weekend. He would arrive in town and either go to her apartment, or accompany her to one of her many jobs. However, Irka would never permit him to sleep at her place, so on every one of those weekend nights, Adam would show up at Hehalutz #9 and throw pebbles at my window. I would come downstairs and open the door for him, and he would spread a blanket on the floor between the two beds and instantly fall into a deep, sound sleep.

Occasionally, I would make the long journey to Jerusalem to visit Adam or to play in a soccer game as a member of the university team. Adam had a parallel community in Jerusalem with a similar group of Polish friends. I could always find him sitting in the corner of Café Brazil on Ben-Yehuda Street with his books strewn about a small table he affectionately called his "office."

Throughout this time, news about the atrocities being

committed in Europe trickled into Palestine. By March 1945, the extent of Hitler's plan to exterminate the Jews had become known. More and more horrific details about Jews being carted away to their deaths flooded the radio waves. As a community, we continued to hope that our families and friends had been spared the violent carnage. The joy of our carefree, bohemian lives in Eretz Israel was tempered by the news from Europe as well as by the increasing Arab attacks on Jewish villages and cities and by our outrage at the immigration quotas and the British refusal to permit the admission of the huge numbers of Jews requesting entry into the country.

Chapter Nineteen

I completed my second year of studies in the spring of 1945, and that summer I took a job as a counselor in a children's day camp operated by a teacher from the Reali elementary school. Every day we organized different and exciting activities for about thirty campers, and every afternoon we brought them safely home to their parents. I enjoyed working with children and felt invigorated by their positive energy. I think I was also relieved to see children immersed in play, untouched by the dismal news of the Nazi atrocities in Europe.

A full-time fourth-grade teaching position became available at the Reali School and I decided to apply for the job. I had some teacher-training from the time I spent in secondary school in Warsaw, but I was not confident of being hired since Hebrew was not my native language. The principal, Emmanuel Yaffe, interviewed me, and after a long conversation, decided to give me a chance at teaching a fourth-grade class. This was a great relief to me because, for reasons I still do not understand, Uncle Sam had abruptly discontinued sending my monthly stipend, and my financial situation had worsened considerably. It was also a relief, because, during the summer of 1945, I started to feel the effects of the war on my emotional state. Everywhere I turned, there was another devastating report indicating that hundreds of thousands of Jews from Poland and the rest of Europe were dead. Spending time with children seemed like a wonderful way of cheering myself up. So I took a leave of absence from the Technion and started teaching. I still continued to take one or two classes, but I reduced my course load significantly, and my sense of satisfaction on receiving my first regular pay check confirmed my feeling that, however temporary, I had made the right decision to work full time.

Mr. Yaffe would occasionally come into my classroom through the back door, but my students were often so completely absorbed in their activities that he would come and go unnoticed. In fact, I remember that there were times when the children and myself were so engrossed in our activities that we would not realize when the school day ended. Mr. Yaffe even received complaints from parents because their children didn't want to leave school until their assignments were complete! These fulfilling afternoons provided me with a great diversion from the terrible news from Europe. While the surviving Jews were being gathered in displaced persons' camps, my students and I were putting on lively Hebrew plays and decorating the school halls with colorful pictures of traditional Jewish holidays. I attempted to keep my students, my classroom, and myself shielded from the realities of war throughout the autumn of that year.

At around the same time, however, I heard that the

Jewish Agency was looking for young people willing and able to travel to Germany to bring orphaned children to Palestine. My experience as a teacher and as a refugee from Poland made me a good candidate, so the Jewish Agency started the process of obtaining a British passport and birth certificate to enable me to travel to Europe. By this time the Agency had mastered the technique of creating identity papers for refugees like myself. The underground contacted the rabbi in Zichron Ya'acov, Rabbi Azrieli, who arranged for my legal papers. He registered my official place of birth as Zichron Ya'acov, Palestine, and changed my name from the Polish *Azrylewicz* to his own. I have used the name *Azrieli* ever since.

Radio reports of the millions of Jews who had perished in the Nazi gas chambers seemed too terrible to be true, but the trickle of European Jews who made their way to Palestine confirmed the existence of these extermination camps. There seemed to be no doubt that my parents and siblings who had remained in Poland had either been killed or were lost somewhere in a displaced persons' camp. Meanwhile, the British patrols kept the borders of Palestine under strict control, and hundreds of surviving Jews who had managed to live to tell about Hitler's "final solution" were still being refused entry to Palestine.

Early in 1946, I became very ill. I have no recollection of the weeks before I fell sick, but some time around December or January I felt exhausted and no longer had the strength to teach or study. With the arrival of each new

141

survivor to Palestine, news circulated about who from Poland was dead and who was still alive. A man from Makow who had survived Auschwitz knew that my mother and sister had been killed soon after they arrived in Birkenau and that my father had been killed after a few months in Auschwitz. This news was simply too much for me to bear. Sapped of all my strength, I simply could no longer continue with my routine of teaching and studying. Until then, hope that my parents and sister had been spared had kept me going. By January 1946, I could no longer deny that any Jewish family that had remained in Poland had been destroyed. With my hope extinguished, I lay on my bed overcome with grief.

Mrs. Shapiro, another teacher at Reali, organized activities with my students and had the children send me colorful get-well cards. After a week with no great improvement, she used her connections and sent me to a convalescent home in Shavei Zion operated by Kupat Holim (the state medical organization). The rest home was situated directly on the ocean and had a trained medical staff. After a couple of weeks, I regained my strength and returned to Haifa. That experience convinced me that I was not in the appropriate emotional condition to assist the Jewish Agency, and I dropped any plans to travel back to Europe.

A few months later, in the spring of 1946, Uncle Nathan wrote to tell me that my brother Ephraim had survived the trials of hard labor in Siberia and was alive in a displaced persons' camp in Germany. My brother wanted to come to Palestine with his wife, Miriam, and their three-year-old son, Motti. I was thrilled to hear that Ephraim and Miriam were alive and amazed to learn that they had had a son in Siberia. I even regained a little hope that Pinchas, or maybe the rest of my family, would soon surface in the aftermath of the war.

During that summer, I used my connections at the Reali School and started my own summer camp. I printed flyers and advertised my day camp to parents from the school and the surrounding neighborhood. There was a tremendous response, and I accumulated about thirty or forty campers. Each day, I took a large group of children to a prearranged outdoor activity. I hired two Egged buses to collect and deliver them at a designated spot every morning and every afternoon. I had so many campers that I even hired two older teachers from the school to help with the activities. We would go to the beach or pool and take hiking trips around the country. I made a substantial profit from this business enterprise, and it was also one of the most enjoyable summers of my life.

With my newly acquired wealth and in response to the oppressively somber mood in the country, I wanted to do something extravagant, so I decided to buy a car! I went to a garage near Tel Aviv and found a 1920s four-door black Riley that had been abandoned by a British officer. It was strewn in pieces all over the garage, but it had once been very beautiful. The dashboard was of wood, with many buttons and gadgets that I had never seen before, like a semi-automatic gear switch located above the steering wheel. I bargained with the owner of the garage and bought it for under £100. I then proceeded, with my limited experience from working at the Ford Motor Company, to put my new possession back together. The interior of the car was completely ruined, so I covered it with an old blanket and, after I got the motor running, I started the long drive back to Haifa. I chugged along the main road between Haifa and Tel Aviv with a rotten exhaust pipe billowing clouds of smoke in my wake. I created quite a scene and a police officer pulled me over — but I didn't care. People in Palestine were lucky to have a bicycle — even Aunt Gonja still rode a donkey to the city — and there I was, driving my very own car! Driving charged me with a new energy, and I loved my new symbol of success and freedom — exhaust fumes and all.

In the fall of 1946, I decided to continue teaching at the Reali School for a second year. Once again, I maintained my official student status at the Technion but renewed my temporary leave of absence. I saw my friends regularly and our conversations frequently revolved around the struggle to create a Jewish homeland. By now, the atrocities committed by Nazi Germany were well known. In response to the annihilation of millions of Jews, establishing a Jewish homeland seemed the only and obvious way of preventing such crimes from ever occurring again.

Normal life continued for my group of friends and, in September, Adam and Irka decided to get married in Jerusalem. Their wedding was planned for Friday, September 13, 1946. I had to teach that morning but, as soon as my class was over, I jumped on a bus from Haifa to

144

Jerusalem, hoping to arrive before the Sabbath. In those days, the trip from Haifa took almost six hours, so by the time I arrived, the ceremony was over but I was still able to dance and celebrate with my closest friend. My gift to the couple was eight pounds toward the purchase of a Hermes manual typewriter, which Adam needed to complete his master's thesis.

The school year progressed and, in February 1947, it was time again for the great Purim ball. My friends and I decorated the backyard of the university with colored balloons and streamers, while other students made masks and costumes. Since the Purim ball was such a great event, Adam and Irka planned to come to Haifa for the festivities. It was during this gala affair that I met Rachel.

Rachel's family was originally from Vienna and had survived the war by living in the south of France. Her brother had been a student at the Technion since 1939 and, after the war, the rest of his family followed him to Palestine. It was only a few months after they arrived that Rachel's brother escorted her to the ball, where I noticed her curly hair, deep brown eyes, and lively intelligent smile. I asked her to dance, and we spent the entire party talking and laughing together. In what seemed like an instant, I fell in love.

Over the next few months, Rachel and I spent wonderful times together. I successfully operated another season of summer camp, and, in my spare time, we took long walks or drives in my car. One day, on our way home from the beach in Nahariya, my car broke down, and we had to leave it by the side of the road near Acre. Even though we had to hitchhike back to Haifa, in the pleasure of Rachel's company, I recall those moments of misadventure as great fun.

Rachel's parents, however, were not very supportive of our romance. Before we met at the Purim ball, Rachel had been dating another man with a permanent and secure job as an Egged bus driver. I was much less established and was developing a desire to spread my wings and see the rest of the world. I wanted to meet my uncles in England and South Africa to try and recreate my lost family. My unwillingness to settle down, coupled with Rachel's parents' influence, contributed to the end of our relationship in the fall of 1947.

With the end of my summer romance, I needed a change. A teaching position opened for an older grade in Pardes Hanna and I decided to take it. I commuted from Haifa every Sunday and returned to my new apartment on Jerusalem Street each Friday, before the Sabbath. The new apartment in Haifa was another sign of my improving financial circumstances, because I finally had enough money to live alone. I even had my very own entrance.

In November 1947, I heard that Ephraim and Miriam had arrived in Palestine and were looking for me at my old apartment on Hehalutz Street. I had kept in contact with Miriam's brother who was living in Rehovot, and I knew they would probably be staying with him. I took the next bus and, after a short time, was reunited with my brother, his wife and my nephew Motti. At once we started planning and devising the best way for Ephraim to earn a living and adjust to life in Palestine. I knew that a course was being offered at the Technion to train new immigrants to work with steel. Ephraim was very good with his hands and already knew how to read structural plans so this seemed like a good course for him to take. I also knew that the Becker family, from my old neighborhood in Haifa, had connections in a steel factory where a job might be available when Ephraim completed the course. Miriam and the baby could stay in Rehovot with her brother, while Ephraim would live in my apartment on Jerusalem Street for the duration of his studies. After he was finished and gainfully employed, the rest of his family would follow him to Haifa.

I kept my job and borrowed Ephraim's bicycle, which he had brought with him on the boat from Germany, to ride between school and my temporary lodging in Pardes Hanna. My busy daily schedule and the deteriorating political situation prevented me from wallowing in my sadness over losing Rachel. The Haganah was making the transition from an illegal underground operation to the official security force of the new Jewish nation. By early spring, many of my friends and I had joined the Haganah and all semblance of regular life stopped.

Not long after Ephraim arrived, the United Nations voted affirmatively on a plan to partition the country and create both an Arab and a Jewish state. In response to this decision, the number of violent Arab attacks throughout the country increased in an attempt to resist the partition. The designated date for the British withdrawal from the country was May 1948.

Chapter Twenty

I started my officer's training course in March 1948, and felt excited and proud to formally participate in the national effort to create a Jewish state. To this day, I consider my small contribution to the war effort as the culmination of my personal fight to survive. The national battle for the creation of the State of Israel was the ultimate fight for survival. Hitler's mass annihilation of the European Jews could not have occurred if a Jewish homeland had existed and been available to provide refuge from his systematic destruction. But, even though I was excited, nothing had prepared me for the feelings of fear and apprehension I also felt as I joined the country's effort in an all-out war, the great war of independence and liberation.

My officer's training course was held in an abandoned British military camp known as "Dora." The camp was located near Netanya and had ready-made barracks for sleeping, a mess hall, and a functioning kitchen. Many Technion students were assigned to Dora to participate in a fast-track military course in preparation for the impending war. Fortunately, the Haganah and the

Anders' army had given me some basic military experience, whereas most of my fellow soldiers had none at all. None of us, however, was familiar with the type of guerrilla warfare that was the pervasive method of Arab attack at that time.

My most powerful memory from my officer's course was on May 14, 1948, the day David Ben-Gurion made the official declaration of independence of the State of Israel. We were gathered in the mess hall anxiously listening to the radio. The camp was in a total blackout, and the windows were covered. Small candles flickered on each table as we silently waited and anxiously listened for Ben-Gurion's voice. The radio announcer continued to give the latest reports of each new attack on Jerusalem and each new threat to our fledgling nation from its Arab neighbors. The threats came from all sides: Transjordan, Egypt, Syria, Iraq, and Lebanon. Collectively, we were filled with anticipation and fear. I believe we were all wondering whether, when the time came, we would be able to sustain ourselves against the well-equipped and better-trained Arab armies.

There was total quiet. The blackened air hung heavily between us as we continued to wait. Finally, after what seemed like ages, Ben-Gurion's voice rang out from the speakers. A Jewish State had been created, he declared, and, in a single instant, the silence erupted into wild cheers.

In the midst of this chaos, a friend of mine climbed on a table and began singing the emotional song *Be'arvot HaNegev*[1] about a soldier who falls during a battle in the Negev desert. He sang, uninterrupted, and we stood frozen and awe-struck as the historic moment was canonized by his voice and the words of this song:

Im tirtzu, chavraiah
ein zu agada

If you will it, friends
It is not a dream

Shiploads of refugees started pouring into the country. People who had survived the intense hardships of World War II were arriving in Palestine and immediately enlisted as soldiers in the army. Units were comprised and commanded by soldiers with little military experience and who spoke many different languages. The abbreviated officer's course at Dora concluded almost immediately upon the declaration of statehood, and I was assigned to a fighting platoon in the newly formed Seventh Brigade.

Our first mission was to try to free the road to Jerusalem, since the city had been completely encircled by the Arab Legion. The single access road to the capital city was blocked, preventing deliveries of medical supplies, food, and water. The entire brigade was sent to Gedera, a little town southwest of the embattled city, where we prepared for our attack. While we waited, terrible *barchash* flies swarmed ceaselessly around our heads, into our eyes, noses, and mouths. Many of us tried to protect our faces with the gauze from our first-aid kits — gauze we would later need in a bloody and exhausting battle.

We finally mobilized at midnight and started our long march to the strategically situated fortress in Latrun. It was pitch black outside, and we were moving through the barren rocky hillside with no clear direction. We lost our way, and, by dawn, we were pinned down and surrounded by Arab soldiers bombarding the hill with sniper fire from all directions. As a unit, we were very disorganized and unprepared for the sniper attacks. In fact, many of us barely knew how to handle a rifle.

As we lay on the hillside, mercilessly beaten, we were unsure about what to do next — some soldiers tried to fight back, while other wounded soldiers could do nothing more than wait for medical assistance. During those long hours, I remember watching my friend from the Technion, Ofer Avisar, distinguish himself by taking command of the troops. He moved from position to position and encouraged us to maintain order; he encouraged us to return fire and to help care for the wounded. Hours later, fellow soldiers broke through the Arab encirclement and helped carry the dead and wounded off the battlefield.

As we were being evacuated, I noticed the oily paper used to wrap shipments of guns strewn over the ground. The army was so desperate for shipments of arms that the guns were being transported directly to the front lines in unopened boxes. Soldiers in a hurry to defend themselves tore the wrappers off these guns and dropped the oily paper while moving toward battle. This is the image that is etched in my mind as we retreated, wounded, dazed, and dehydrated.

★

In the late 1980s, *The Jerusalem Post* printed an article about a young woman who was the sole survivor of her family and had come to Palestine after the war. She became a communications officer in the army and had exhibited great heroism by insisting on being on the frontlines in the battles of Latrun. Her commitment stemmed not only from her courage and readiness to die for a Jewish homeland, but also from her belief that she was all alone in the world. During one of those bloody battles, she was killed. Not long after her death, her mother, who had in fact survived the war, came to Israel in search of her daughter — but it was too late.

Reading this heartbreaking story, I recalled my own involvement in the fight for Latrun. I decided to contact (Ret.) General Shlomo Shamir who, I was told, was writing a history of these battles. When I first met the General, he was reluctant to talk to me. Apparently, many people had claimed involvement in these battles and he was skeptical of my story. He asked me many questions, and, after an extensive examination, he finally pulled out his war documents. I was specifically interested in regaining contact with Ofer. Over the years I had forgotten his last name, but I had never forgotten the courage he had exhibited on that hillside near Latrun. Shamir found my name on the list of soldiers who had served in the Seventh Brigade, and he also found the name of Ofer Avisar, who, I was thrilled to learn, was alive and working as an engineer in Haifa.

I contacted my old friend, and we were reunited. At our first meeting, I was again deeply impressed by the courage Ofer continued to show in his every movement. Ofer had been twice wounded as a soldier in heroic battles for the State of Israel. Today, he is physically handicapped, but his positive approach to life had not changed at all over the years. It was a great pleasure to meet him again. A few years after our reunion, Ofer and some other veterans became interested in building an amphitheater for the use and enjoyment of the Seventh Brigade in the Golan Heights. I decided to get actively involved in sponsoring this project, and Ofer was instrumental in seeing to its successful completion. Near the amphitheater is a building that contains a memorial for all of the soldiers who fell in the battles of Latrun. It is located near Katzrin and has been actively used by soldiers since May, 1995.

After our initial, unsuccessful attack on Latrun, military intelligence reformulated the strategy of how to gain control of the road to Jerusalem. A few days later, the Israeli forces conducted a military operation that opened an alternate passage to Jerusalem, permitting the transport of supplies and medical personnel. I was recuperating from minor wounds and dehydration in a medical facility and only heard about the army's success over the radio.

In July 1948, I was transferred to the air force and assigned a position as an Officer of Education and Welfare.

153

My responsibilities involved formulating programs for educational and cultural events in the north of the country. As a city officer, I was afforded the luxury of living in my own apartment on Jerusalem Street while working in a downtown office. I was responsible for the welfare of air-force soldiers, arranging for their care when injured and making official visits, on the army's behalf, to their families. I was also required to organize activities intended to inspire the morale of the soldiers. I spent time creating a library of magazines and periodicals, and I also interviewed and hired musicians and artists to perform at military bases. To this day, the healing effect that beautiful music has on a disheartened or wounded soldier has never ceased to amaze me.

In September 1949, I was officially discharged from the army and started thinking about my next step out into the world. I had resumed regular contact with my uncles in South Africa and England and was eager to meet them. I craved the kind of support that I thought I could find in my extended family — and I also craved the adventure of visiting other countries. Through the Jewish Agency, I found a job as a youth leader in Cape Town, South Africa. The Jewish community was looking for a Hebrew-speaking teacher and I considered this a welcome opportunity to see the world and visit Uncle Sam in Johannesburg.

In February 1950, I packed my belongings and left some sentimental items with Ephraim, like my soccer shoes and drafting table. I bought a plane ticket to South Africa (with stops in Khartoum and Nairobi) on a new Israeli passenger DC–3 aircraft. The morning my flight was scheduled to depart, there was a rare snowstorm in Tel Aviv. Although there had been an accident on an airplane traveling from England to Israel earlier that day due to the harsh weather conditions, we still boarded the plane at the scheduled time and sat on the runway while the ground crew brushed the accumulating snow from the airplane wings. By the time one wing was cleared, the other was covered in snow. After what seemed like many hours, the plane took off into the snowy skies. I was headed toward a new continent and a new chapter in my life.

1   "In the Negev Desert," by Rafael Klazkin.

Epilogue

There has been an ongoing debate among my friends and family about whether this memoir should focus solely on my life until 1950, or whether Danna and I should continue our collaborative effort to include my experiences thereafter. I feel that ending the story in 1950 is appropriate, as it marks the conclusion of the first phase of my life. Clearly this phase had a most significant impact on my life after 1950. The story of my later adult life, I am confident, will also be told in its own time.

My escape from Poland, the home I had known until 1939, was forcibly dictated by the war. My arrival in Eretz Israel (in 1942) and my participation in the struggle to establish the State of Israel reflected a dream that I had harbored since childhood. After witnessing the establishment of a Jewish homeland, I was secure in the knowledge that other Jews would no longer have to experience the persecution that I and millions of others had known.

After the creation of the Jewish homeland, it was time for me to take steps to fulfill another dream: to see the world. In my mind, my pre-war life in Poland seemed to be

157

a distant memory. My turbulent adolescence and my feverish young adulthood had been characterized by a continuous struggle — first to stay alive, and then to reach Palestine. Now I could finally act upon my desire to see and experience what the world had to offer. I had always been curious and eager for new experiences. I approached each new city or town with much enthusiasm and wonder. My travels to South Africa, England, Western Europe, and North America enabled me to overcome some of the feelings of rage and sense of loss that the war had fostered in me. I was able to move forward and start over, focusing on the present and the future.

Yet, my love for Israel was my beacon, giving me the courage and strength to continue my journey through life, especially when I felt at times that my inner resources were depleted and challenged. When I boarded the plane that dramatic and snowy afternoon in Tel Aviv, I vowed to return when I would be in a position to make a real contribution to the country. Wherever I traveled, and wherever fate brought me, I always kept the thought of Israel in my mind. The desire to contribute to Israel, to give back to the homeland that had given me so much pride, was a vow I made to myself. Therefore, regardless of where I went, I knew that the experiences gained along the way would enrich whatever contribution I would eventually make to Israel.

After many voyages, I settled in Montreal, Canada, where I met my wife, Stephanie. Together we raised four children: Rafi, Sharon, Naomi, and Danna. My life in Canada, between 1954 and the late 1980s, provided me with a range of experiences and expertise. I had wonderful opportunities to design and build various buildings, including shopping malls and office complexes in Canada, the United States, and Israel, thereby putting into practice my lifelong love of design and architecture. Canada's tolerance and open multiculturalism provided a unique and most supportive environment for all my evolving dreams and endeavors. I was fortunate to participate in Canadian and Jewish community life and to contribute to educational and other philanthropic organizations, including the Canadian Zionist Federation, which elected me its national president. I received numerous honorary degrees and I was especially honored to have been named to the Order of Canada in 1984. I also finally found the time, at age 75, to go back to school and continue my dream of studying architecture, graduating with a Master's degree in architecture in 1997.

It is said that a man is a reflection of his homeland, but sometimes a man has more than one homeland. Both Israel and Canada helped forge my identity and sense of belonging, and in recent years I have been able to bring much of what I learned in Canada to Israel, with beneficial results. Thus, in 1982 I was fortunate to begin my first business venture in Israel, in Ramat Gan, north of Tel Aviv, where I purchased a tract of land that no one wanted, near a small but congested intersection. I designed and built the first enclosed shopping mall in the country, which I hoped would bring retailers and consumers to enrich the economy. In my wildest dreams, I never anticipated that this mall and the others I later completed in Beersheva in 1990, and in Jerusalem in 1993, would achieve the kind of success they did. They helped bring new ideas in merchandising, distribution, financing, and customer service to Israel. As of this writing, I am in the process of completing the Azrieli Center in Tel Aviv, which I consider to be my crowning achievement. The shopping mall phase of the project opened officially in April 1998 to crowds far exceeding my wildest expectations.

I have been blessed to have had the opportunity to focus on what I love to do in the places that I love most — to build and design in Israel and Canada. This passion for my work and for my homelands is what has led to my success.

To my wife and children, who have always given me their support, their steadfast trust, faith, unconditional love and encouragement, I extend my eternal appreciation.

A special thanks to my daughter Danna for writing this story. Her natural curiosity and avid interest in my journey and her heritage, provided her with the sustenance and inspiration to persevere and produce so eloquent a work.

David J. Azrieli

July 2001